ON LEGISLATURES

ON POLITICS

L. Sandy Maisel, Series Editor

On Politics is a series of short reflections by major scholars on key subfields within political science. Books in the series are personal and practical as well as informed by years of scholarship and deliberation. General readers who want a considered overview of a field as well as students who need a launching platform for new research will find these books a good place to start. Designed for personal libraries as well as student backpacks, these smart books are small format, easy reading, aesthetically pleasing, and affordable.

Series editor L. Sandy Maisel is the William R. Kenan Jr. Professor of Government and is Director of the Goldfarb Center for Public Affairs and Civic Engagement at Colby College. He is also the director of the Colby in Washington Program.

Books in the Series
On the Presidency, Thomas E. Cronin
On Appreciating Congress, Louis Fisher
On Foreign Policy, Alexander L. George
On Thinking Institutionally, Hugh Heclo
On Legislatures, Gerhard Loewenberg
On Ordinary Heroes and American Democracy,
    Gerald M. Pomper

Forthcoming in the Series
On Media and Making Sense of Politics, Doris A. Graber

GERHARD LOEWENBERG

ON LEGISLATURES
The Puzzle of Representation

Paradigm Publishers
Boulder • London

Copyright © 2011 by Paradigm Publishers

Published in the United States by Paradigm Publishers, 2845 Wilderness Place, Boulder, CO 80301 USA.

Paradigm Publishers is the trade name of Birkenkamp & Company, LLC, Dean Birkenkamp, President and Publisher.

Library of Congress Cataloging-in-Publication Data

Loewenberg, Gerhard.
    On legislatures : the puzzle of representation / Gerhard Loewenberg.
        p. cm. — (On politics)
    Includes bibliographical references and index.
    ISBN 978-1-59451-751-8 (hardcover : alk paper) —
    ISBN 978-1-59451-752-5 (paperback : alk paper)
    1. Representative government and representation. 2. Legislative bodies.
I. Title.
    JF511.L598 2010
    328.3—dc22
                            2010020952

Printed and bound in the United States of America on acid-free paper that meets the standards of the American National Standard for Permanence of Paper for Printed Library Materials.

Designed and Typeset by Cheryl Hoffman.

15 14 13 12 11   5 4 3 2 1

CONTENTS

PREFACE

I have been thinking and writing about legislatures throughout my entire professional career. I therefore welcomed the invitation from Jennifer Knerr of Paradigm Publishers and L. Sandy Maisel of Colby College to write a book about legislatures for their innovative series On Politics.

Despite the large literature on legislatures, there are surprisingly few general books on this important political institution. This book is intended for students of legislatures in undergraduate courses and as an introduction for graduate students interested in the subject. I hope it will also appeal to those members of the public who care about democratic politics but are baffled from time to time by the peculiarities of this venerable institution.

Legislatures seem to have the characteristics of other things we love: we can't live with them but we can't live without them. I aim to explain what makes legislatures so puzzling and to sketch in broad outline what has been learned about them as a result of the large volume of research since the middle of the last century.

I am indebted to many colleagues who have over the years continued my education in the field of legislative research. In writing this book, I have particularly valued the advice of Peverill Squire, who read the entire manuscript, made many valuable suggestions, and saved me from making numerous errors. The chapter on representation was improved by the careful reading given it by Stephen Ellenburg. Douglas Dion straightened me out regarding some aspects of chapter 5, "Ways of Studying Legislatures," for which I am very grateful.

For over half of my professional life, I have worked with Michelle L. Wiegand in editing the *Legislative Studies Quarterly*. I could not possibly have had a more loyal, more supportive, and at the same time more exacting colleague. Editing the journal made it possible for me to maintain my knowledge of the literature of legislative research even when other responsibilities at the University of Iowa might have distracted me.

My wife, Ina, encouraged me to write this book and read the entire manuscript. Her sense of style and the logical development of ideas greatly improved the manuscript as well as everything I have ever written.

CHAPTER ONE
LEGISLATURES AS PUZZLES

Legislatures are puzzling institutions. How is it that a collection of several hundred members who are nominally equal to each other can ever reach a decision? How is it that an institution, which is presumably representative of the people, is usually the most unpopular institution in a system of government? These contradictions arise out of the history of the institution, out of the contrast between the characteristics it had at its origin in medieval Europe—its genetic properties, so to speak—and those the institution developed as it adapted to changing political environments over eight or nine centuries. It would be difficult to imagine any other organization of several hundred members that had no boss, no assignment of duties, no one in charge of hiring or firing, and no "bottom line" to evaluate success or failure. Legislatures attract scholarly attention, in part, because they are puzzling. Interested citizens who look at sessions of a legislature on public television usually see numbingly boring scenes of members speaking to an empty chamber, or standing around waiting for the results of a roll call, or interrupting each other with points of order. It is hard to make any sense of what is going on.

Legislatures are unlike other political institutions, most of which can be pictured on an organizational chart with defined lines of authority and responsibility. By contrast, each member of a legislature is formally equal to every other member; no member can legally order another member around, let alone hire or fire him or her. No constituency can accept control of its representative by a representative of another constituency. So legislatures are large collections of individuals who do not formally owe each other obedience and do not necessarily accept any division of labor among themselves. No wonder legislatures are difficult to understand. And no wonder they so often frustrate the public by their apparent indecisiveness. How they manage to act at all is one of the central puzzles that scholars have tried to understand.

Legislatures as Objects of Research

Legislatures multiplied in the second half of the twentieth century with the multiplication of independent countries. By the first decade of the twenty-first century, there were 191 national legislatures, as well as a very large number of legislatures at sub- and supranational levels of government.[1] Their role in their political systems varies enormously. A bold recent effort to assess the influence of 158 of these legislatures in their respective countries measures thirty-two aspects of their constitutional powers derived from expert opinions and legal texts and compares the power of the legislature with that of the executive. By that measure the U.S. Congress, generally regarded by legislative specialists as the most powerful legislature in the world, comes out in forty-ninth place.[2] The survey is obviously a rough effort, its results providing evidence of the difficulty of assessing the role that legislatures play in governance by relying merely on expert opinions of legal texts.

A few legislatures can trace their origins back over a thousand years, among them the Althing of Iceland, which first convened in AD 930, marking the beginning of the Icelandic Commonwealth. It was originally an outdoor gathering, open to all free men, in which the country's most powerful leaders declared law and settled disputes. An example at the other end of the long history of parliaments is the National Council of Slovakia, established in 1993 when Slovakia became an independent state after the peaceful dissolution of the Czechoslovakian federation. Its 150 members exercise veto-proof legislative powers, have considerable oversight capacity, and can dismiss the government by a vote of no confidence. Although a relatively new parliament, the council has assumed an assertive political role similar to that of the older, but recently democratized, legislatures of Central and Eastern Europe. The Kenyan National Assembly, established in 1963 upon the independence of that country from the United Kingdom, is typical of the new parliaments in sub-Saharan Africa, which have only very slowly been able to assert some independence from powerful executive rulers. Among the weakest parliaments are such appointed bodies as the Consultative Council of Saudi Arabia. One of the strongest legislatures in the twenty-first century is the German Bundestag, heir to a checkered history growing out of its beginnings in an authoritarian, newly united state in the nineteenth century, an unsuccessful democratic interval after World War I, and a remarkably successful new beginning after the end of the Allied occupation of the country.

These examples illustrate the puzzling variety that exists among legislatures. Some of them, including the more powerful ones, have existed in one form or another since medieval times, when monarchs first summoned representatives of medieval communities to confer with them on matters of war and peace and raising governmental revenue. Some of the more powerful ones are of more recent origin, notably in Europe and in the states formerly belonging to the British Empire. Many of the newest legislatures—those in the Middle East, North Africa, the post-Soviet states, and Southeast Asia—are among the weakest. But their age does not seem to relate to their role in the political system; nor does their size, their location, or their organization. As puzzling as their variety is their near universality. Despite widespread public despair over them, legislatures exist in nearly every political system in the world.

They all have in common their structure—they are assemblies of nominal equals—and their reason for being—they are at minimum consultative bodies for rulers. Governments of all kinds seem to require their existence. Publics of all kinds seem to regard them as objects of despair.

Legislatures are very feasible subjects of study. Typically they are accessible, they are relatively open to researchers, they document their actions, and their members are willing—often eager—to talk about what they do. Early legislatures have often left extensive records of their work. Thus, many examples can be studied. Legislatures attract country and area specialists. As legislative institutions have achieved prominence in international organizations, they have also attracted a significant body of scholarship, for example, in studies of the European Parliament. Legislatures attract scholars who are interested not in the institution as such but in political developments with which legislatures are connected, notably the modernization of traditional societies in what Samuel Huntington called the third wave of democratization.[3]

The overwhelming amount of research on the U.S. Congress is the product of the very large group of American government specialists in political science, for whom Congress has been a central object of research from the earliest days of the organized profession, beginning with Woodrow Wilson's *Congressional Government* published in 1885.[4]

Research began to proliferate after 1945. Congressional studies became a subspecialty in American political science, formatively shaped by a few influential scholars, including Ralph Huitt at the University of Wisconsin; David Truman at Columbia University; Donald R. Matthews at the University of North Carolina, Chapel Hill; Nelson Polsby at the University of California, Berkeley; Richard F. Fenno Jr. at the University of Rochester; and David Mayhew at Yale University.[5] They and their students, encouraged and aided by the Congressional Fellowship Program established by the American Political Science Association in 1953 and by the organization of accessible data on Congress, created a community of students of Congress that has no counterpart in legislative studies in any other country. The strength of this group of scholars is that it has produced an array of research methods and research agendas that have been gradually applied to the study of other legislatures. But for nearly half a century, the study of Congress completely outdistanced the study of legislatures outside the United States, both by American and by non-American political scientists. Legislative research was therefore predominantly research on the institution in its American historical and cultural context, which shaped both the research methods that developed in this field and the conceptualization of the subject.

Studies of legislatures in other countries were, like congressional research, country specific. In the last twenty years, however, there are increasing examples of cross-national legislative research in explicitly comparative frameworks. This has made it possible to get a better general understanding of the legislature apart from its specific manifestation in a particular country or at a particular time. Rational-choice theory has proven to be especially suitable for this purpose because it focuses on institutional structure independent of cultural-historical contexts. International contacts among scholars have facilitated this development. For example, the consolidation of democracy in Latin America has led specialists in Latin American politics to undertake extensive research both on individual legislatures and on sets of legislatures in a comparative framework.[6] I will discuss many other recent examples of comparative research on aspects of legislatures in subsequent chapters.

Because many legislatures are of long standing, they have attracted historians, particularly in Great Britain and on the European continent. Under the aegis of the History of Parliament Trust, set up in 1940, British historians have published twenty-eight volumes covering 281 years of parliamentary history, including 17,000 biographies of members.[7] In 1936 a group of European scholars organized the International Commission for the History of Representative and Parliamentary Institutions, which has published a broad range of historical studies of parliamentary institutions for over seventy years. It is an active scholarly organization with two hundred members in thirty countries, meets annually, and since 1981 has published the journal *Parliaments, Estates & Representation*.[8] Originally an organization of medieval historians focused on the history of parliamentary institutions in Western Europe in the Middle Ages, it has in the last two decades broadened its purview to include articles and monographs on parliaments up to the present, covering all of Europe and often taking a comparative approach. With the revival of interest in the German parliamentary tradition after World War II, German historians established a commission in 1952 to sponsor research on the development of German parliaments, which has resulted in 250 monographs and volumes of primary documents.[9]

Unfortunately, there is little interdisciplinary work on legislatures. There are exceptions, notably the work of the historian William O. Aydelotte. His analysis of the British House of Commons of 1841 to 1847 reflected his interest in the application of quantitative methods to the history of legislative behavior and led him to organize interdisciplinary conferences bringing together historians and political scientists doing legislative research.[10] But political scientists rarely avail themselves of the research of historians, be they American, British, or continental European. In turn, British and European historians are seldom aware of the research of American political scientists, even research that pertains to the early history of American legislatures. This is only one of several examples of barriers that divide scholars in the field of legislative studies by disciplines and by country.

As research subjects, legislatures have proven suitable to successive methodological fashions in the discipline of political science: legal-constitutional analyses of their rules and powers, sociological analyses of their memberships, attitudinal surveys of their members' policy preferences and role concepts, participant observation of their members' activities, and game-theoretical interpretations of how they reach decisions. Legislative research has escaped the methodological controversies that exist in many subfields of political science because over time each of these methods of study has helped to illuminate the characteristics of legislatures.

In its many manifestations, legislative studies constitute a thriving field of research. Venues for publishing legislative research in political science have multiplied in the last half century, beginning with the British journal *Parliamentary Affairs* in 1947, the German journal *Zeitschrift für Parlamentsfragen* in 1969, the *Legislative Studies Quarterly* in 1976, and the *Journal of Legislative Studies* in 1995. However, neither the general public nor politically attentive publics nor scholars in neighboring fields share the fascination for legislatures that exists among students of legislatures in political science. Public attention to legislatures occurs chiefly when they are involved in scandals or fail to act promptly on a political issue that the public wants resolved. Then they are generally disparaged. Voters may have a positive view of their representative in a legislature but that does not translate into regard for the institution. One of the most notable legislative scholars, Richard F. Fenno Jr., once asked why "we love our congressmen so much more than our Congress."[11] That is one of the many puzzles that scholars have tried to understand. The institution that is designed to represent the public has long been the object of public criticism and ridicule. The famous caricature by Honoré Daumier, showing overfed, complacent members sitting in the French parliament in 1834, illustrates that the merciless depiction of legislators is nothing new (see Figure 1.1). It could be duplicated by political cartoons going back to the eighteenth century in the United States and Europe, as well as by cartoons of the present day.

Historical Evolution of Legislatures: Structural Adaptation in the American Context

The antecedents of the modern legislature lie in the feudal assemblies of medieval, precapitalistic, predemocratic Europe.[12] On the continent of Europe, significant examples existed in the form of

Figure 1.1 Honoré Daumier print: "The Legislative Paunch, 1834" (The Legislative Belly, 1834 [litho] by Honoré Daumier [1808–79] Private Collection/ Courtesy of Swann Auction Galleries/ The Bridgeman Art Library)

provincial assemblies on the subnational as well as the national level. Monarchs convened assemblies of feudal lords irregularly when they needed these powerful individuals for money and for military conscripts. These assemblies were not intended to govern but merely to consult, to *parler* with monarchs. Three basic characteristics of what we now call a legislature can be traced to its origins. From its beginnings the institution was, first, an assembly of influential people who occasionally had the opportunity to give or withhold consent to the monarch. Second, the members of the institution represented others, such as social classes or local communities, and this determined who was selected to be a member, how individuals were selected, and how many were selected. And third, the members bargained with the monarch, exchanging consent to the monarch's wishes for legal favors for their constituents. The more frequently these assemblies met, the more they devised procedures that would enable such a group of proud and powerful individuals to reach collective decisions. Thus, assemblies of feudal lords were transformed into parliaments, but not yet—not nearly yet—into democratic parliaments.[13] The genetic properties of legislatures—that they are a collection of influential people, that they represent others, and that they bargain with the government on behalf of their constituents—have made them distinctive political institutions, recognizable in all their subsequent manifestations but not easily understood. Adapting these characteristics to modern, democratic politics creates the puzzling contradictions that legislatures display.

The transformation of this basically medieval institution into a democratic one began in colonial America in the seventeenth and eighteenth centuries. The assemblies established in each of the thirteen American colonies proved ideal instruments for contesting British authority.[14] Of all the political institutions in the colonies, they alone were not appointed by the British government. Composed of colonists, they could claim to represent the interest of the colonies against the Crown. In the century and a half of their development before the American Revolution, these assemblies provided their members experience with working within the institution, with developing rules and structures that made it feasible to reach collective decisions. The process of their institutionalization was so far advanced by the time of the American Revolution that at the point of independence, the thirteen American states created state legislatures in the image of the colonial assemblies that had gone before. The Congress established by the Constitution of 1789 bears many of the marks of the colonial legislative experience as well. The lineage of American legislatures shows a remarkable continuity. From the beginning they were separate from the executive branch of government. From the beginning they asserted lawmaking powers. Their committee structure, their officers, their procedures, and their norms of behavior reflected their assertion of an independent role in the system of government. They had a well-defined shape as political institutions by the time the expansion of the suffrage in the early nineteenth century made it possible to describe them as democratic institutions.[15]

Historical Evolution of Legislatures:
Modernization in the European Context

In Europe, where this medieval institution originated, the process of its modernization and democratization followed a different path. The contest with royal authority was not one with a remote ruler but with an ever-present executive. Challenging the legitimacy of royal authority was more complicated than the assertion of a desire for political independence, as the American colonists had argued it. It required questioning royal authority on its home ground and opposing to it the will of an emerging bourgeoisie, which asserted itself in Great Britain first in the Revolution of 1688. A century and a half later, it led to a series of reforms in the system of selecting the members of Parliament. Comparable electoral reforms occurred on somewhat different timetables throughout Europe, gradually changing the composition of parliaments to reflect the changing social composition of industrializing nations. The modernization and democratization of the institution through this process of changing its composition reshaped its relationship to the executive in a manner quite different from the way that relationship developed in North, and later in South, America. The British approach was to assert the supremacy of Parliament and to constrain the traditional prerogatives of the monarch by imposing on the monarch's ministers the will of the leaders of the majority in Parliament. With the expansion of the suffrage, that parliamentary majority was gradually linked to the political parties outside Parliament that organized the growing electorate. This meant that the European development of parliaments was driven by political parties, which, among other things, democratized the recruitment of members of parliament. Universal manhood suffrage existed in all European countries by the end of the nineteenth century; women's suffrage followed with, on the average, a half century's delay.

The result of the European path of the development of legislatures was either to circumscribe the powers of the monarch, as in Great Britain, or to overthrow the monarchy, as in France and much later in Germany. In either case its result was a complex fusion of executive-legislative powers regulated by constitutions written or, in the case of Great Britain, unwritten. In the fusion of executive-legislative powers, political parties played a decisive role. Where a single party could attain a majority in parliament, its leaders became the effective holders of executive power by being able to control parliamentary decisions.

Walter Bagehot, the first British editor of the influential weekly *The Economist*, offered the first politically realistic analysis of the English constitution as it had developed in the nineteenth century.[16] He argued that the British parliament was only an electoral college, which chose a cabinet, which in turn governed the country. Monarchy, he observed, was merely theatrical window dressing. Bagehot's analysis inspired Woodrow Wilson's research on Congress twenty years later, in which he concluded that American government realistically seen was congressional government and that within Congress the committees held dominant power.[17]

Where no party could attain a majority, as in most of continental Europe, executive power was dispersed among the parliamentary leaders of several parties who attempted to govern in coalition with each other. This gave parliaments more influence on the conduct of government than they had in Great Britain, since the making and breaking of coalitions required frequent negotiation among the parliamentary parties involved. In that somewhat inscrutable and often time-consuming process, the balance of legislative-executive power depended less on the constitution than on the internal organization of the political parties, which could vary from one party to another and did not readily lead to a stable equilibrium among the parties. As a result, governing coalitions were often unstable. The contradictions that arose in the various phases of adapting a medieval institution to a modern political environment struck European writers profoundly. Some were distressed by the threat to executive authority posed by parliaments, some regretted their rapidly changing social composition, and some were alarmed by the growing influence of political parties on their decisions. James Bryce, historian and member of the British parliament from 1880 to 1907, gave classic expression to this dismay in the chapter entitled "The Decline of Legislatures" in his two-volume *Modern Democracies*.[18] He was nostalgic for a "golden age of Parliament" that had presumably existed before the expansion of the franchise beyond the propertied middle class. In a passage that still resonates today, nearly a century later, Bryce wrote,

> Every traveller who, curious in political affairs, enquires in the countries which he visits how their legislative bodies are working, receives from the elder men the same discouraging answer. They tell him, in terms much the same everywhere, that there is less brilliant speaking than in the days of their own youth, that the tone of manners has declined, that the best citizens are less disposed to enter the Chamber, that its proceedings are less fully reported and excite less interest, that a seat in it confers less social status, and that, for one reason or another, the respect felt for it has waned.

Bryce observed that "the spirit of democratic equality has made the masses of the people less deferential to the class whence legislators used to be drawn," that "the personal qualities of a candidate do less to commend him to electors who are apt to vote at the bidding of party," that legislators "set little store by the standards of decorum that prevailed when . . . two generations ago, a large proportion of the Chamber belonged to the same cultivated social circles," and that "the disappearance of this sense of social responsibility has affected the conduct of business" so that "every rule of procedure, every technicality is now insisted upon and 'worked for all it is worth.'" What summed up these changes for Bryce was that "parliamentary deliberations seem more and more of a game, and less and less a consultation by the leaders of the nation on matters of public welfare."[19] In referring to parliamentary deliberations as a game, Bryce was perhaps prescient: Half a century after he wrote, a new generation of political scientists conceptualized parliamentary procedure as a competition capable of being explained in game-theoretical terms.

Bryce was by no means alone in expressing disillusionment with parliaments. The rise of political parties had distressed the Federalists in the United States as early as the beginning of the nineteenth century. Throughout the nineteenth and early twentieth centuries, it was a recurring theme on both sides of the Atlantic that party caucuses dominated the decisions of legislatures operating from outside the institution. British, French, and German writers repeatedly wrote on this theme, the most influential being the Russian-born political sociologist Moisei Ostrogorski, who published a frequently cited work titled *Democracy and the Organization of Political Parties* (originally in French) in 1902.[20] Other writers, notably Max Weber in Germany and Robert Michels in Italy, compared the waning influence of parliaments with the power of party oligarchies, interest groups, the popular press, and expanding bureaucracies.[21]

Four Puzzles of Legislatures

So, in the American environment, the medieval parliament became a legislative assembly separate from the executive, while in the European environment it became a deliberative assembly related to the executive in a variety of ways that were shaped by party systems. Both developmental paths left contradictions between the inherited structure and the modern political environment, the source of persistent puzzles about the modern legislature.

Puzzle 1: Representativeness

The first puzzle concerns the representativeness of the modern legislature's membership. Originally monarchs managed the appointment of members. Later members were chosen in the territorially defined constituencies by a very limited franchise, reflecting the influence of the landed gentry. Eventually they were chosen by an ever-widening electorate organized by political parties. The membership of legislatures therefore kept changing, reflecting changes in society filtered by electoral systems. These changes were continuously accompanied by controversy over whether the membership was representative of the nation. Representativeness has always been a defining characteristic of legislatures, but its meaning has always carried an element of uncertainty. The myth persisted in most European parliamentary systems that at one time members were independent of interests and parties, guided only by their sense of the general welfare, and that the independent gentleman member was the standard by which members should forever be evaluated. The more realistic assessment of the composition of legislatures related it to the social and ethnic structure of the country and to the professionalization of politics. One of the most influential studies of the membership of the British parliament as it was at the time of the American Revolution demonstrated that members reflected and served the local interests of their constituencies and that they had no more general ideological or partisan objectives.[22] The membership of contemporary legislatures consists increasingly of professional politicians who manage to convert the mandate into a sinecure; voters tend to view them with suspicion and cannot in any case identify with them. That raises new questions about the representativeness of legislatures and about the electoral systems that select members and secure their reelection. It also prompts proposals for increasing membership turnover.

Puzzle 2: Organization and Procedure for Assemblies of Equals

The second puzzle about legislatures concerns the inconsistency between the organizational and procedural structures they have developed and the original notion of an assemblage of notables of equal status. From a remarkably early point in their history, legislatures organized committees. Ivor Jennings, in his classic work *Parliament*, notes that "the institution of the select committee, consisting of a few members nominated for some specific purpose, goes back to the earliest times of which records exist."[23] The colonial assemblies had standing committees to handle recurring important matters, and the committee systems in some of the larger states were quite complex by the middle of the eighteenth century.[24] The need to get work done drove legislatures to this method of delegation to subgroups of their members. Until the beginning of the twentieth century, however, the British parliament, sensitive to the right of every member to consider every important bill with reference to the interests of his or her constituency, resisted the establishment of standing legislative committees with definite jurisdictions as opposed to select committees for specific purposes. Until 1907 all general legislation was considered in committees of the whole house, using a procedure more flexible than that which existed on the floor. Only the appearance of minority obstruction and the increasing complexity of legislation finally made the establishment of standing committees indispensable. Legislatures vary greatly with respect to the power and number of their committees, from the extensive committee system of the U.S. Congress to the limited committee structures in Great Britain and France. Despite this wide variance in the number of committees, the tension persists between the desirability of specialized competence in the legislative process and the appeal of enabling every member to participate equally in that process.

Legislatures are, among other things, social organizations. Their members group themselves partly by geographic, religious, occupational, and ethnic affinities. They also form friendship groups and develop social patterns out of their life at the seat of the legislature, where they take their meals and where they live. The rooming houses of Washington, D.C., in the early 1800s shaped political ties among members of Congress,[25] as the coffeehouses of London, Paris, and Berlin shaped political factions in their respective parliaments. Seating arrangements within legislatures both reflect and reinforce friendship groups. Well before the expansion of the suffrage, members of legislatures grouped themselves by their political loyalties, forming what James Madison condemned as "the violence of faction."[26] With the expansion of the suffrage, party organizations became indispensable for organizing the electorate, and these extraparliamentary party organizations inevitably developed ties to party groupings within the legislature. The relative influence of the extra- and intralegislative organization of political parties has spawned a large body of scholarship, both normative and empirical. Undisputed is the fact that political parties are as indispensable to the organization of modern legislatures as are their committee systems. If we recognize that the subjects of legislation are bound to be controversial, the division of the membership by parties should not be surprising wherever parliaments allow the open expression of opinion. But partisanship remains a bad word—just as its older counterpart, factionalism, once was—out of nostalgia for the "independent" member motivated only by the general welfare. Just what reality this concept might have, or might ever have had, is still another puzzle in the study of legislatures.

Over the centuries of their existence, legislatures gained experience with the processes that could enable them to reach decisions. Experience showed that

- members' speech needed protection but also limits

- the rights of minorities needed protection from the majority

- taking a legislative proposal in the form of a bill to a decision in the form of an enactment required agreement on sequential stages of consideration

- the rules governing the process required stability and impartial application by a presiding officer

- the relations among members required the acceptance of norms of behavior that reduced personal conflict and promoted interpersonal trust

An understanding of these characteristics of legislative procedure is the province of specialists, the so-called clerks or parliamentarians that all modern legislatures employ.

Many aspects of the legislative process are the product of experience; therefore, much of legislative procedure takes the form of precedents, akin to judicial precedents in common law countries, rather than of explicit rules. Because of the importance of experience, parliamentary procedure has been borrowed over time by newer from older legislatures, from one country to another. These borrowings can seem at first indispensable to a new legislature; yet, in practice the details may be perplexing to the borrower. To the uninitiated outside observer, they may forever be inscrutable. When as vice president from 1797 to 1801 Thomas Jefferson presided over the U.S. Senate, he felt obliged to compile *A Manual of Parliamentary Practice*,[27] in which he borrowed heavily from a four-volume compilation of the *Precedents of Proceedings in the House of Commons* published in 1718 by a clerk of the Commons, John Hatsell.[28] Jefferson's *Manual* eventually became a supplement to the rules of procedure that evolved in the U.S. House of Representatives and in territorial and state legislatures throughout the United States. To the outsider parliamentary procedure is mysterious. On the surface, many of the ways in which legislatures proceed defy common sense, appear tedious, require of members insincere deference to those with whom they disagree, and seem hypocritical.

Puzzle 3: The Role of Legislatures in the Political System

The third puzzle concerns the appropriate role of the legislature in the political system. That is reflected in the variety of names given to the institution across the world. The most common name refers to the structure of the institution as an assembly of members. That is the meaning of *Majlis* (a place of sitting, in Arabic) and *Knesset* (a place of gathering, in Hebrew), the terms used in Arabic countries and in Israel, respectively. In Germanic countries, the term *Diet* (*Tag*) has been used, meaning "day of meeting," so that Bundestag literally means the "day of the federation." The next most frequent name refers to the institution's deliberative activity, its function as a place to talk, to *parler*. The name *Duma*, which is used to designate the lower house of the Russian parliament, means "to think or consider." The term *legislature* is used officially to designate the national institution or one of its two chambers in only five instances in the world today—Costa Rica, El Salvador, Samoa, Tonga, and Uzbekistan. In bicameral parliaments, the name for the directly elected chamber usually refers to its representative character, while the name of the indirectly elected or appointed chamber predominantly uses the term *Senate*, the name of the ancient

Table 1.1 Names of Legislatures

Unicameral (114)			
National Assembly	63	Council	8
Parliament	24	Congress	5
Chamber of Deputies or		Legislative Assembly	4
House of Representatives	6	Other	4
Bicameral (77)			
Lower chamber			
Chamber of Deputies	43	House of Commons	1
National Assembly		Legislative Chamber	1
or Assembly	22	Duma	1
Congress	4	Knesset	1
Diet	4		
Upper chamber			
Senate	50	Lords, Elders	2
Council, Councilors	8	Other	6
Council of States	11		

Roman assembly, which meant "an assembly of elders" (see Table 1.1).

The medieval assembly was originally a consultative body. It could challenge monarchical decisions and demand attention to its petitions, but it did not presume to govern. The role of the British parliament grew in the sixteenth century during the reign of the Tudors, when its assent to legislation and appropriations became indispensable. The term *legislature* first appeared at the end of the seventeenth century in England, derived from the noun "legislator," meaning lawgiver. When you look up "legislature" in the *Oxford English Dictionary*, the first reference is to Matthew Hale's *History of Common Law*, which asserts that "without the concurrent Consent of all Three Parts of the Legislature, no . . . law . . . can be made."[29] The phrase "all Three Parts of the Legislature" refers to the House of Lords, the House of Commons, and the king. These three together were the lawgivers. Using the term *legislature* to apply only to Parliament resulted from a mid-eighteenth-century normative theory that it was desirable to separate the powers of government, a theory most notably developed by the French political philosopher Montesquieu.

After the term *legislature* was applied only to Parliament, it crossed the Atlantic, where Montesquieu's advocacy of the separation of powers suited the colonists especially well. In *The Federalist* #47 on the separation of powers, Madison repeatedly cited "the celebrated Montesquieu." The term *legislature* then became the common word for the colonial assemblies in America, because by asserting lawmaking powers, these assemblies could challenge British control. The word shows up as early as 1712 in reference to the New York assembly, which is discussed as a part of the legislature.[30] Beginning in the nineteenth century, it was used to refer to representative assemblies in the presidential systems of Latin America, but elsewhere the representative assembly is not usually called a legislature. Although I use it as a generic term to denote all variants of this institution, as I have indicated, the name of the institution varies from one country to another.

To the extent they were influenced by the role of Parliament in Great Britain, the colonial assemblies in America asserted the right to initiate legislation and revenue measures, but they were primarily motivated by the desire to offset the policies of the colonial governors appointed by the Crown. In the decade before the Revolution, these assemblies became the dominant institutions in the colonial system of government, increasingly challenging the parent British government. That set the precedent for the role of legislatures in the independent American states, where the original constitutions provided for "legislative supremacy," and in the national political system that followed, where it was entrenched in the written constitutions of the states and the federal government. The provisions for a Congress possessing "all legislative powers" delegated to the national government had pride of place as the first article of the U.S. Constitution. In Europe, by contrast, such a clear separation between the roles of the legislature and of the other institutions of government was not established, so the role of the legislature varied to a greater extent, from one country to another and from time to time, than it did in the United States. Nelson Polsby, one of the foremost students of legislatures in the second half of the twentieth century, regarded the differences among legislatures as lying along a continuum from those that were actively "transformative" of governmental decisions to those that were mere "arenas" for deliberation. "At one end," he wrote, "lie legislatures that possess the independent capacity . . . to mould and transform proposals, from whatever source, into laws." At the other end lie arenas, Polsby wrote, which "serve as formalized settings for the interplay of significant political forces," but the existence of arenas "leaves unanswered the question of where the power actually resides that expresses itself in legislative acts." Polsby wrote that "the contrast between arenas and transformative legislatures captures many of the differences that scholars customarily note in their discussions of the two great legislatures on which legislatures in most of the rest of the world are modeled—the British and the American."[31]

The difference between Polsby's two types becomes visible architecturally when one compares the British House of Commons, in which two sets of benches face each other and which has an insufficient number of seats for all its members, to the U.S. House of Representatives, which has seats and desks for every member, arranged in a partial semicircle. One is a debating chamber, the other a place where legislative details can be discussed. When it came time to rebuild the House of Commons, after it had been damaged by a bomb in World War II, Winston Churchill, who loved the House, recognized that the floor of the chamber was usually empty. He therefore insisted, to everyone's surprise, that it be rebuilt exactly as it had been, far too small to seat all its members. "If the House is big enough to contain all its members [Churchill explained] nine-tenths of its debates will be conducted in the depressing atmosphere of an almost empty or half-empty chamber."[32]

The contrast between the chamber of the U.S. House of Representatives and the chamber of the British House of Commons illustrates the puzzling difference between the role of the legislature in these two political systems (see Figures 1.2 and 1.3).

Puzzle 4: Making Legislatures Understandable

Perhaps the greatest puzzle that legislatures present is how they can be made comprehensible to the wider publics they are supposed to represent. Legislatures are simply uncommon organizations. They are distinct from the more familiar institutions of politics, from executive bureaucracies, from courts, from political parties, and from interest groups. Each of these can be pictured as hierarchies; none of them requires anguishing considerations of representativeness, purports to be transparent, or exhibits internal controversies so blatantly. How legislatures work has few analogies to organizations familiar to outsiders. Although the institution bears the marks of its medieval origins, it is strikingly widespread in the world today. Many influential

Figure 1.2 Floor of the British House of Commons (Deryc R Sands © Parliamentary Copyright)

Figure 1.3 U.S. House of Representatives (Office of Photography, U.S. House of Representatives)

observers in and outside of the discipline of political science echo what Bryce called "the pathology of legislatures."

Unraveling the puzzle of legislatures is not a trivial undertaking. It has attracted respectful attention in the relevant academic disciplines and occasionally from informed observers outside the academy, who are at times cynical as well. In the chapters that follow, I explore the principal puzzles outlined here, the puzzles of representation, organization and procedure, and the legislature's role in the political system. I return at the end to that most baffling, but also most important, puzzle of all: how to make the legislature understandable to the public it is designed to represent.

CHAPTER TWO
REPRESENTATION

Concern with representation has existed since the Middle Ages, if not earlier. The concept of representation is difficult to clarify, but it is so intimately related to a legislative institution that it is bound to appear and reappear in the study of legislatures. Political power in medieval Europe was divided among the monarch, the servants of the monarch who constituted the administration, the nobility, and a number of cohesive social groups—the landowners, clergy, and leading citizens of the towns. Communication among these geographically scattered holders of power was difficult but necessary if anything like government for the territory was to function. Under these circumstances monarchs in all the major European countries would summon members of the leading social groups to their palaces for consultation. These assemblies were the precursors of parliaments. One of the foremost students of medieval parliaments has written,

> In the corporative and feudal society of the Middle Ages, everyone was subject to precise limitations. . . . But what no individual vassal could do, parliament was able to, through the fiction that it represented the entire country. . . . [Parliament] gave reality to the terms "country," "land," "patria," "people," "kingdom," "the community of subjects," which hitherto had existed as mere

abstractions or figures of speech. Through parliament these abstractions came to life, and by their vote gave royal decisions unlimited authority and the moral support of "consent."[1]

Medieval parliaments, modern European parliaments, the U.S. Congress, and legislatures in developing countries all have in common their claim that they stand for the nation. That claim has had different justifications at different times and in different cultural settings. It meant one thing in medieval status societies, something else in the agricultural societies of predemocratic colonial America, something else again in the class-based societies of democratizing Europe in the nineteenth century, and something different still in the process of democratization in the United States and later in other parts of the world.

The Meanings of Representation

An unusually fruitful interplay between theory and empirical research on representation in the last half century has helped to disentangle its various meanings and to apply them to explorations of legislative behavior. Much recent theoretical work on representation relies on the writing of Hanna Pitkin, who used ordinary language philosophy to explore the concept of representation's historical meanings and to suggest what it means today.

Etymologically, as Pitkin put it so tantalizingly, representation means "the making present in some sense of something which is nevertheless not present literally or in fact."[2] The Latin word was not originally used in any political context. It did not begin to be attached to a political relationship until the Middle Ages when, by way of Catholic theology, it referred first to the personification by a living individual of someone or something else, for instance, the pope representing Christ. Later, it referred to a legal agent acting for a collectivity or another person. The term *representation* did not become explicitly attached to parliament, the political institution for which it ultimately became a defining characteristic, until late in the sixteenth century, about three centuries after that institution began to develop in England. At first, the term *representation* had been used in its symbolic sense to describe parliament as standing for the nation. In the period leading up to the English civil war, it began to be used in its more active sense to describe the fact that parliament acted for the nation. In its literal meaning, the term *representation* is clearly paradoxical: It makes something present that is not really present. This intrinsic paradox has made it suitable for describing the complex political relationship between those who govern and those who are governed. Pitkin clarified the concept of representation by tracing the accumulation of its meanings from Thomas Hobbes to Edmund Burke and into contemporary usage. She distinguished between the use of representation to mean popular authorization of authority, as in Hobbes, and to mean accountability, as in later liberal thought. She explored the controversy between those who believed a representative was a delegate or mere instrument of his constituents and those who believed he was a trustee obliged to use his own judgment, a controversy first elaborated by Burke in his address to his constituency in Bristol, England:

> Certainly, gentlemen, it ought to be the happiness and glory of a representative to live in the strictest union, the closest correspondence, and the most unreserved communication with his constituents. Their wishes ought to have great weight with him; their opinion, high respect; their business, unremitted attention. It is his duty to sacrifice his repose, his pleasures, his satisfactions, to theirs; and above all, ever, and in all cases, to prefer their interest to his own. But his unbiased opinion, his mature judgment, his enlightened conscience, he ought not to sacrifice to you, to any man, or to any set of men living. These he does not derive from your pleasure; no, nor from the law and the constitution. They are a trust from Providence, for the abuse of which he is deeply answerable. Your representative owes you, not his industry only, but his judgment; and he betrays, instead of serving you, if he sacrifices it to your opinion.

Burke did not persuade his constituency. He had developed his views of representation as a member of Parliament for a small, rural constituency, but a rising industrial constituency like Bristol expected its member to be more of a delegate of their interest, and he lost his seat.[3] Although he did not resolve the puzzle of representation for himself, his concept of representation as a dichotomy between trusteeship and delegation has persisted.

Descriptive Representation

Pitkin contrasted representation in its descriptive, symbolic, and active senses. In its descriptive sense, representation refers to the composition of a legislature and regards a legislature as representative if its members mirror the population in those respects that are salient to a community, such as social class, occupation, race, ethnicity, and gender. The underlying assumption is that a legislature representative in these respects will act in a manner consistent with the interests of these elements of the community. This concept of representation has prompted a large body of research on the composition of legislatures and the recruitment processes that influence their composition, especially in the class-conscious European scholarly communities.[4] The result has been an extensive mapping of the changing demographic—specifically social-class—composition of European parliaments from the predemocratic parliaments through the effect of the expansion of the suffrage beginning in the middle of the nineteenth century and continuing to the present. There has also been a special interest in the changing occupational composition of legislatures in the process of industrialization, which gradually resulted in the replacement of farmers and landowners by businessmen and white-collar professionals and by labor union and church officials, with the occupational distribution varying by parties. The occupations of members of European, Latin American, and Asian parliaments differ considerably from one party to another and display a more varied composition than does the U.S. Congress.

A distinguishing characteristic of American legislatures in the twentieth century was the predominance of lawyers, who constituted half of the members of the House of Representatives and two-thirds of the members of the U.S. Senate as late as the 1970s, a far larger proportion than in other parliaments. But the increasing professionalization of politics has changed the composition of Congress and of most U.S. state legislatures. In the first decade of the twenty-first century, one-third of the members of Congress come from public service or political backgrounds and an equal third come from business; now little more than one-third have had prior occupations in law, and only one-fourth continue to have occupations related to law.[5] Similar developments in Europe, in those legislatures like the U.S. Congress that meet steadily throughout the year, have by now everywhere produced a political class that is, and appears to the public to be, clearly unrepresentative of its constituents. This discrepancy is one source of public distrust of legislatures: The public does not recognize itself in its representatives occupying increasingly professionalized legislatures. This explains at least a part of the puzzle that the most explicitly representative institution in political systems is usually the most distrusted by those it is supposed to represent. In the newer legislatures of eastern Europe, Africa, and Asia, where there have been only one or two generations of members of freely elected parliaments, identifiable political careers are only gradually emerging. The comparison of the occupational composition of legislatures presented in Table 2.1 illustrates the variation that exists, but the difficulty of comparing occupations across countries limits the validity of precise comparisons.

In the United States there has been a particular concern with descriptive representation with respect to the gender and racial composition of legislatures. The remarkably slow growth in the proportion of women in American legislatures compared to those in other countries reveals that the single-member-constituency system of elections is an obstacle to the entry of previously unrepresented social groups. The proportion of

Table 2.1 Occupations of Legislators

	Percent of Members Whose Occupations Are Related to						
Legislature	Law	Education	Other Professions	Business	Farming	Political Occupations	Others
Anglo-American							
U.S. House of Representatives	26	13	–	30	1	31	–
UK House of Commons	12	15	13	32	1	19	9
New Zealand House of Representatives	15	14	18	16	8	28	2
Western European							
Austria National Council	11	11	17	15	9	22	15
Denmark Parliament	6	10	19	11	2	35	17
France National Assembly	8	14	19	23	3	15	18
Germany Bundestag	18	7	33	3	2	19	16
Switzerland National Council	15	8	13	25	12	22	9
Eastern European							
Hungary National Assembly	22	17	24	19	6	5	7
Poland Sejm	12	14	30	21	5	15	3
Ukraine Parliament	19	12	43	18	4	0	4
Latin American							
Argentina Chamber of Deputies	25	11	17	12	8	2	25
Chile Chamber of Deputies	28	11	29	13	8	3	9
Asian							
India House of the People	8	6	37	15	28	2	4

Source: Inter-parliamentary Union; Jennifer E. Manning, *Congressional Research Service Report* #40086 (February 4, 2010): "Membership of the 111th Congress: A Profile."

women in the legislature is much larger in countries using systems of proportional representation, in which each constituency elects a multiplicity of members, making it possible for parties to nominate "balanced tickets." But the electoral system is not all that matters. Cultural expectations also influence receptivity to representation by women. Change over time is not steady: From the time of women's eligibility for election, after the beginning of the twentieth century, to the present, the increase in the proportion of women has not been linear or steady. A line showing the proportion of women in legislatures over time shows only a slow increase at first, then a more rapid rise, and then a leveling off short of the proportion of women in the population.[6] The proportion of women in the U.S. Congress had reached only 5 percent by 1989; twenty years later women constituted 17 percent of the membership, more than a threefold increase but one that leaves women still in a small minority.[7] Among major democracies using systems of proportional representation, the proportion of women in legislatures is much larger. In the small countries of northern Europe, women now make up around 40 percent of the membership of parliament; in Spain, Belgium, New Zealand, and Germany, over 33 percent of the members are women.[8]

A different obstacle exists to the representation of racial and ethnic minorities in U.S. legislatures. Assuming that voters are influenced by the race of the candidate, the supposition has been that single-member constituencies will elect an African American or Latino candidate only if there are concentrations of such ethnic groups in the legislative constituencies. With the goal of increasing minority representation, Congress in 1982 amended the 1965 Voting Rights Act to mandate that minorities be able to "elect representatives of their choice" by permitting the creation of a series of "minority-majority" districts, that is, districts deliberately so drawn that a majority of their population consists of a racial minority.[9] This change led to a 50 percent increase in the number of African American members of Congress and also to a very gradual increase in Latino members. But these changes also led to a series of successful court challenges that restricted the extent to which explicit racially motivated districting was permissible under the law. The proportion of African Americans in the U.S. Congress reached 4 percent of the membership in 1989, and twenty years later it was twice that proportion, still only two-thirds of the group's proportion in the population.

The connection between electoral processes and the composition of legislatures has produced some general conclusions, notably, that the size of constituencies—"district magnitude"— is the critical variable in linking the social composition of the electorate to the composition of the legislature. This means that proportional representation with large multimember districts is more likely to lead to legislatures that mirror the salient characteristics of the population than small districts or, at the low end of district magnitude, single-member constituencies. This linkage is mediated, however, by many intervening variables, notably the supply of candidates, cultural expectations, the proportion of incumbents and challengers, their styles of campaigning, and decision-making processes within legislatures themselves that affect districting and other aspects of the electoral process. Electoral systems cannot easily be imposed on legislatures from the outside, although courts and popular initiatives have occasionally compelled changes in existing systems. But legislatures mostly determine their own electoral systems. Therefore, the status quo is not readily altered.

How far the social composition of legislatures affects their actions has recently been the subject of a growing body of research. Implicit in the concern for descriptive representation in legislatures is the assumption that demography is destiny, that the social background of members determines their actions and affects constituents' satisfaction with representation.[10] But it is by no means clear that gender or ethnicity or other aspects of the social backgrounds of legislators determine their decisions, or when or on what matters their social identities affect their decisions. Social identity does affect the initiatives members take in the legislature, the bills they propose, the committees on which they serve, and the subjects on which they speak, but social identity is not clearly evident in the votes on the wide range of issues taken by legislators.

Symbolic Representation

Distinct from descriptive representation is symbolic representation in the sense that the legislature stands for the community and the community recognizes itself in the institution. As symbols can evoke emotions and attitudes, so a legislature can be perceived as representative or unrepresentative. Representation in this sense is a matter of attitude, both of the community toward the institution and of the members of the institution toward the community. Recognizing this aspect of representation explains the puzzle that legislatures devote a great deal of time to actions that appear to have no practical purpose, particularly those that are primarily ceremonial or ritualistic. John C. Wahlke, looking at the distribution of time spent in the Iowa legislature two generations ago, concluded,

> A considerable amount of legislative energy appears to be spent in activities serving mainly to generate goodwill and diffuse support in largely symbolic fashion. Proposals granting or seeking symbolic recognition of community values, such as a resolution (not adopted!) memorializing Congress to designate the corn tassel the national floral emblem, are only one variety. . . . Spreading on the record . . . readings . . . of moralistic, hortatory, or other value-diffusing poetry and literature is another. But the most common activity serving to generate diffuse support among constituents and the wider state public is the public introduction of distinguished, and often not so distinguished, visitors in the gallery to the House.[11]

What Wahlke observed in the Iowa legislature a generation ago occurs and reoccurs in all legislatures, often to the bafflement of observers, and becomes a source of cynicism for all but those being courted. Although it would appear to be the most abstract aspect of representation, symbolic representation finds a specific application in the contribution that legislatures make to nation building, to giving a set of separate communities the sense that they belong together as a nation. Indeed, providing a sense of national identity was one of the original functions of the parliaments of medieval European states, and it remains an important function of parliaments in developing countries today.

Active Representation

In its active sense, representation refers to acting for others, as an agent acts on behalf or in place of another. In the last decade, representation studies have used the concept of agency to explore the link between representatives and the represented. Regarding the represented as the principals and representatives as their agents provides a framework for exploring those activities of legislatures that serve specific constituency demands for specific services and the allocation of specific goods. Extensive research exists on "constituency errands," on the circumstances in which members of legislatures serve the specific demands of their constituents. The conclusion from this line of research is that "service responsiveness" is a ubiquitous function of legislatures in all political systems, although its magnitude varies.

The principal-agent approach to the study of representation is less appropriate to those deliberative policy-making activities of legislatures that exhibit an interactive relationship between the representative and the represented. Michael Mezey points out in his study *Representative Democracy* that "empirical research on representation . . . suggests that representatives play a significant role in *shaping the views of their constituents.*"[12] The policy responsiveness of legislatures cannot be assessed on a single issue at a single moment in time. It is a linkage relationship that emerges over time as legislators and constituents—individually and collectively—listen to one another, consider what each is saying, and answer each other, though not necessarily by affirming each other's will. As we shall see, it is the most complicated aspect of representation to study empirically.

Instead of choosing among the diverse meanings of representation—descriptive, symbolic, and active—Hanna Pitkin tried to discover their common core. She suggested that in politics, representation does not denote a relationship among individuals, or even between an individual and a collectivity, but between two collectivities: constituencies and the institutions that act for them. Thus, "political representation is primarily a public, institutionalized arrangement involving many people and groups, and operating in the complex ways of large-scale social arrangements." And "within a state, representation most commonly is ascribed to the legislature." She summarized her view in these words: "Representing . . . means acting in the interest of the represented, in a manner responsive to them."[13] Note that she referred to the "interest" of the represented, not the "interests"— in other words, to a collective good, not an array of individual goods. Note also that she regarded representation as a public, institutionalized relationship, not a one-on-one relationship. By this definition empirical research on representation is very challenging. Yet, clearly it is very important to try to determine when a legislature acts in a manner that is representative of its constituents and when it is unrepresentative.

Clarifying the Delegate-Trustee Dichotomy

Although Pitkin's work has been highly influential in all research on representation for over forty years, work on conceptual clarification of representation has continued, addressed particularly to unpacking Burke's dichotomous distinction between the relationship of trustee and delegate into a more complex set of relationships. That distinction has repeatedly appeared in empirical research because it promises insight into the puzzle of what constitutes a representative action of an individual legislator or of the collective legislature. Andrew Rehfeld has pointed out that the representative relationship raises three independent questions: Should representatives pursue the good of the whole or of a part, should they rely on their own judgment or the judgment of their constituency, and should they be responsive to their constituency regardless of their own views? Since each of these three questions has two possible answers, Rehfeld posits eight possible representative relationships rather than two: 2 x 2 x 2.[14] His set of ideal types accommodates the diverse functions of representative legislators—their deliberative functions as well as their constituency-errand functions—more effectively than the trustee-delegate dichotomy, which obscures many normative concerns. By distinguishing between the aims of a representative (good of the whole, good of the part), the sources of the representative's judgment (self or others), and the responsiveness of the representative (independent or subject to sanction), Rehfeld can imagine a trustee instructed by his constituents to use his own judgment as well as an independent delegate choosing to follow his constituency's wishes. While the instructed trustee and the independent delegate appear to be paradoxical types of representatives, difficult to observe, these types may come close to how many representatives actually behave.

Empirical Research on Representation in U.S. Legislatures

Scholarly work on representation has profited from the fact that the last half century has seen one of those surprisingly rare intersections between work in traditional political theory—of which Pitkin's work is an exemplar—and contemporary empirical research, which was blooming in the 1960s under the influence of sociological theory and the "behavioral persuasion" in political science. Conceptual clarification has, however, raced ahead of empirical research. Initially, empirical research did not get beyond the delegate-trustee dichotomy. It focused on two observables: legislators' conceptions of their representative role, as measured through interview studies, and responsiveness, defined as congruence between the views of constituents measured by survey research and the votes of their representatives measured by roll call data. Such data existed or could be obtained easily in the American setting, and its availability facilitated research.

Two studies published in the early 1960s became paradigmatic in research on representation, both influenced by the behavioral persuasion in political science, to which I return when I discuss the methodology of legislative research in chapter 5. The first was a comparative study of legislators' conceptions of their representative role, based on parallel interviews conducted in four American state legislatures. John C. Wahlke, Heinz Eulau, William Buchanan, and Leroy C. Ferguson examined what they called the "representational role orientations of legislators." Influenced by sociological role theory, the authors conceptualized the legislature as a system of roles among which the representative role was central.[15] They distinguished between the geographic focus of legislators' representational roles and their style of representation, be it delegate, trustee, or a mixture they called "politico."[16] Their findings were largely descriptive, mapping the way members of American state legislators conceptualized what they were doing as representatives. It provided a building block but did not really unravel the puzzle of what constitutes a representative action.

The second paradigmatic study was likewise influenced by the behavioral persuasion in political science. It took off from studies of the roll call voting behavior of members of Congress and sought to identify the relationship between constituency opinion and members' votes. Warren E. Miller and Donald E. Stokes' 1963 article titled "Constituency Influence in Congress"[17] was pathbreaking because it related the prodigious volume of roll call studies of legislative behavior, which had had a long tradition of research on Congress, to the increasingly important survey research on the voting behavior of the public. Their diamond-shaped diagram, which pictured the relationships between the attitude of the constituency, the attitude of the member, the member's perception of the constituency, and the member's roll call vote, shaped empirical research on representation for a generation after their article was published (see Figure 2.1).

Miller and Stokes concluded that in the late 1950s, when their data were gathered, members of Congress acted as delegates of their constituencies on civil rights issues on which public opinion was presumably well developed, as partisans on social welfare issues on which party divisions were clear, and most nearly as trustees on foreign policy issues.[18] The role-theoretic approach used in the Wahlke et al. study of representation was followed for about two decades in the United States and longer in other countries, but its shortcoming was that it explained only what legislators thought they were doing rather than what they actually did. Its attractions were that the data required were readily obtainable by interview studies and that the trustee–delegate dichotomy seemed to translate well into a wide variety of national settings. The Miller and Stokes approach has had a longer life, despite two fundamental shortcomings, one empirical and the other conceptual. The empirical problem is that samples of constituency opinion are bound to be small, no matter how large the national sample of public opinion from which constituency samples are drawn. The original Miller and Stokes study had to divide a national probability sample of less than two thousand respondents by 116 constituencies, leaving an average constituency sample of just seventeen respondents. The authors were well aware of the reliability problem this limitation

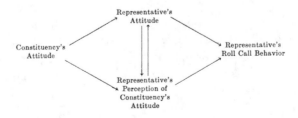

Figure 2.1 Connections between a constituency's attitude and its Representative's roll call behavior

raised, a problem that subsequent studies could not escape. The conceptual problem goes beyond the problem of reliability of small samples and leaves several puzzles unresolved. What is the equivalence between voters' policy preferences, which are likely to be general, and the specific actions on particular bills that legislators take? Is congruence between these two very different indicators of preferences all that is needed to assume perfect representation? Further, is constituency opinion merely the sum of the attitudes of all its citizens at one moment? Can one merely add up the opinions of individuals in a constituency consisting of hundreds of thousands of voters—whose attitudes might be sharply divided, might be vague or unformed depending on the issue, or might be unstable—and regard that sum as the constituency's opinion?[19] And do constituents actually have well-formed opinions on many issues faced by representatives?

Conceptualizing constituency attitudes as a sum of individual attitudes and legislators' actions as the record of roll call votes was rooted in the micropolitical approach prompted by the behavioral persuasion in political science, which tended to focus research on the actions of individual voters and individual legislators, rather than on the collective preferences of groups of voters and the actions of legislatures as collectivities. It overlooked Pitkin's view that representation is a relationship between legislatures and constituencies conceptualized as collectivities, not a relationship among individuals. It also failed to examine more complex representational relationships than the Burkean trustee-delegate dichotomy. Legislators may well regard themselves as representatives of the interests of subconstituencies, which are narrower than the interests of their entire geographic constituency. They may also regard themselves as representatives of regional or national interest groups that cut across many geographic constituencies. Furthermore, they may well regard their representational roles as going beyond roll call voting on one proposal at a time. Representation is, after all, a dynamic relationship that emerges over time as events develop and as representatives interact with each other and with their constituents.[20] This dynamic aspect of representation becomes apparent in any case study of the evolution of a policy proposal in a legislature, which often takes place over many months or years. The legislator is not merely the object of fixed constituency opinion but is active in shaping that opinion as the policy proposal undergoes modification through the stages of the legislative process. Finally, legislators must make constant assessments of the intensity with which their constituencies feel the issues, and they must respond accordingly. In extensive research on members' differential participation in the committees and on the floor of Congress, Robert L. Hall concludes that members' assessments of the intensity of their constituents' opinions guide "the day-to-day decisions [about] how best to allocate the time, energy, and other resources of their enterprise on the numerous issues that arise both within and beyond the panels to which they are assigned."[21]

Heinz Eulau, coinvestigator of the role-theoretic study of representation, showed the most sensitive awareness of the fact that legislatures have collective properties that are not the mere aggregations of the properties of their individual members, or of their role concepts, or of their roll call votes. That awareness led him to an effort over many years to clarify the methodological problems entailed in the empirical analysis of such collective properties of legislatures as their representational linkages. I return to a more general discussion of what Eulau called the "micro-macro dilemma" when I discuss the methodology of legislative research in chapter 5. But Eulau tackled the specific challenge of studying representation empirically by taking an approach out of Plato's *Republic*, believing that large units might best be studied in their smallest manifestations. With his student Kenneth Prewitt, Eulau designed a study of eighty-two three-, four-, and five-member city councils and analyzed their aggregate properties. The book resulting from this project was neglected in the discipline, falling in the gap between the fields of local politics, small group studies, and policy analysis.[22] It deserves more attention in the discipline than it received. Consistent with Pitkin, Eulau and

Prewitt recognized that the analysis of representation "should direct attention to representation as a property of the collectivity rather than as an attribute of individual persons."[23] They measured that property by constructing it from observations conducted, first of all, at levels other than that of whole councils, namely, interviews with council members, which they coded for members' expressed attentiveness to constituents' demands, to particular groups in the community, and to "attentive publics." They then transformed their interview data into data on group properties, which was feasible for these small legislatures having only three to five members each. Their analysis of the correlates of responsiveness could achieve reliable results because of the exceptionally large number of legislatures—eighty-two—in the study. Although a study of a set of city councils in one American urban area may not provide a template for other studies of representation, it exhibited a standard of methodological sophistication that has been largely forgotten.

Cross-National Research on Representation

While Eulau's work was increasingly theoretical and methodological, the expansion of interest in representation from work on American legislatures to empirical work on legislatures in other countries also contributed sensitivity to the appropriate units of observation other than individual legislators and single-member constituencies. To the extent that studies of representation focused on American politics, the constituency of members was bound to be the geographically defined district. For example, David Mayhew interpreted congressional behavior in terms of the "electoral connection" between members and their constituencies and concluded that congressional organization was ideally suited to its members' reelection ambitions.[24] In his highly influential set of participant observations on the "home style" of members of the House of Representatives, Richard F. Fenno Jr. depicted how members of Congress perceive their constituencies in four concentric circles, beginning with the geographic constituency and proceeding then to ever smaller circles: the reelection constituency of the members' supporting voters, the primary constituency of supporting party members, and finally the personal constituency of the members' friends.[25]

But when one looks at representation in the context of legislatures with multimember constituencies and strongly disciplined parties, within societies exhibiting sharp social, ethnic, and cultural cleavages, the inadequacy of a focus on individual members, individual voters, and single-member constituencies becomes apparent. To unravel the puzzle of what the representativeness of legislatures means in a broader perspective has required attention to two kinds of collectivities: political parties and multimember constituencies. Gary C. Jacobson could interpret many of the characteristics of the U.S. Congress, including the long periods of one-party dominance and the frequency of "divided government," in terms of the politics of the U.S. single-member-constituency electoral system.[26] Outside the United States, on the other hand, relatively cohesive political parties, able to impose voting discipline on the members of their parties in legislatures, make the party an inescapable unit of observation in the representational linkage. Furthermore, the prevalence of proportional representation requires attention to the collective interests of large, multimember constituencies. Empirical work has proceeded on the assumption that in countries with multiple, cohesive parties, constituents' preferences can be measured by their choice of political parties in elections, and the policy preferences of legislators likewise can be measured by their party affiliation. Representation then depends on how effectively given electoral systems translate voters' party preferences into the partisan distribution of legislative seats. This approach to representation has led to research on the political consequences of the different electoral systems that developed in the twentieth century.

The single-member-constituency systems used in the United Kingdom, the United States, in much of the English-speaking world, and in the former British colonies originated in medieval societies consisting of geographically separate communities. Paradoxically, this system became widely used in modern dictatorships because it is so easily manipulated in the process of drawing district lines and nominating candidates. It therefore lends itself to the maintenance of one-party domination. The combination of its use in the English-speaking world and in one-party dictatorships leaves this originally medieval system in use in nearly one-fourth of the countries of the world, many of them with large populations in Africa, Asia, and North America, so that two-fifths of the world's population lives under this system.

At the beginning of the twentieth century, single-member constituencies became questionable as an instrument of representation in what were becoming industrial societies with mass publics, societies that spawned a multiplicity of political parties. In three-quarters of the democratic countries of the world, some variant of proportional representation, often a hybrid that includes single-member constituencies, is now dominant.[27] Comparative research on representation accordingly focuses on such a system.

If representation means responsiveness to the collective interest of the constituency, the size of the constituency affects representation in two ways. The larger the constituency, the more difficult it is to aggregate the interests of its citizens, although large multimember constituencies can be represented by a set of members exhibiting a broad range of its interests. The smaller the constituency, the larger the number of constituencies the national legislature must accommodate, and each constituency can only be represented by a single member or a very small set of members. The existence of a large number of single-member constituencies poses a collective-action dilemma, which occurs when the self-interests of individuals add up to the detriment of the general interest. This is most readily demonstrated by legislative decisions on appropriations. Individual legislators are each tempted to support spending in their own districts and are in turn prepared to support the spending proposals of their colleagues, all of them knowing that the costs of each of their proposals is not borne by their district but distributed across all districts in the national budget. The result is "pork-barrel spending" and "earmarking," those much criticized tendencies observed in the appropriations process of the U.S. Congress, but not only there. By contrast, proportional-representation systems, with their relatively large multimember constituencies, reduce this temptation and are likely to support spending decisions that produce broader collective benefits. A growing body of research has begun to test the political consequences of variation in electoral systems, with findings that suggest that proportional-representation systems result in legislative decisions favoring income redistribution, stronger governments, and appropriations for more public goods.[28]

Determining the role of political parties in the representational linkage requires evidence that party voting by the electorate reflects voters' policy preferences and that legislators' votes on policy reflect those preferences. In the 1970s and 1980s, a series of studies applied the Miller and Stokes congruence model of representation to a succession of legislatures in Europe, including the Netherlands, France, Sweden, and Germany. However, the model did not fit well with electoral systems having multimember constituencies or lead to those general insights into representational linkages that Miller and his colleagues sought.[29] The effort to develop cross-national findings on representational linkages therefore took a different turn in the last decade of the twentieth century by focusing on the role of political parties in the representational linkage. Although there has been no single comparative study of policy representation in which political parties are the representational linkages, ten separate studies conducted in five countries showed how electoral systems affect the way parties link the legislator to the constituents. These studies examined the relationship between two sets of collectivities: between the median *party* voter and the median *party* member of the legislature, and between the median voter and the median member of the legislature without regard to party. The cross-national conclusion is that responsive-ness to the median voter without regard to party is better in majoritarian electoral systems, while responsiveness to party vot-ers is better in proportional systems. Furthermore, the more parties in a system, the greater the responsiveness to party voters. This cross-national research therefore shows how significantly political parties link legislators and their constituents, especially in proportional-representation electoral systems.[30]

There have also been efforts to determine how far voters hold well-defined policy preferences at all, how much these preferences vary from one issue to another, and whether a uni-dimensional measure of voter preferences, most commonly represented by a left-right scale, can capture attitudes toward multidimensional issues.[31] This research shows that voter prefer-ences are clearest on those overriding "superissues" that are reflected in the left-right distinction in European political sys-tems and the liberal-conservative distinction in the United States, like issues of social welfare and taxation. But not all issues boil down to this single dimension.

The focus on party and policy in comparative studies of representation takes account of the reality of party-organized legislatures and party influence on voting behavior. Its short-coming is the ambiguity of party as an indicator of policy and the vagueness of the average voters' issue preference on most issues before the legislature. The strength of the focus on party representation is that it recognizes that both electorates and leg-islatures consist of sets not of separate individuals but of collectivities, and in that respect this focus is on representation as Pitkin conceptualizes it.

Measures of Legislators' Preferences

Still another approach to research on legislative representation is to explain the decisions of legislatures in representational terms not by the mere sum of the separate votes of each member on individual issues but by an ordering of each member's votes on all issues expressed as that member's "ideal preferences." The availability of roll call data for all U.S. Congresses beginning in 1789, together with the development of powerful supercomputers, created the temptation to infer members' positions—their "ideal points"—on a single policy dimension, thinking in geometric terms as Anthony Downs had suggested in his pathbreaking *An Economic Theory of Democracy*.[32] Downs had posited that when political issues divide voters and politicians on a single dimension from left to right, then there will likely be a normal distribution of voters and politicians along a line from left to right with a single peak near the midpoint. The simplicity of this conception made it very attractive. Keith Poole and Howard Rosenthal used it to represent the positions of members of Congress from 1789 to the present in such a unidimensional geometric space. On that basis they computed scores measuring members' positions on roll call votes for all Congresses and made the data available to all scholars. The result was a large body of research that shares a common set of measures, which the authors called NOMINATE. The measures rest on a common set of assumptions about legislators' preferences derived from their votes.[33] Roll call analysis therefore became a minor industry in U.S. congressional research because of the availability of roll call data for the entire history of the U.S. Congress, the development of spatial models of voting that enabled scholars to identify the dimensions of legislators' preferences from their individual votes, and advances in computer technology that permitted the analysis of very large bodies of data.

Because most of this research dealt with a single legislature, the U.S. House of Representatives, the effect of the institutional setting on the voting record was long neglected. Research did not take into account that the policy positions of legislators cannot always be read merely from their votes on the final passage of legislation. Many important decisions are made without calling the roll. Furthermore, in many of the world's legislatures, recorded votes are rare. Cross-national research has made clear that the validity of roll call votes as a measure of legislators' policy preferences cannot be assumed. The voting record, always incomplete even in the United States, is governed by rules of procedure that differ from one legislature to another, and even within a legislature, such rules differ over time. The record is also affected by various incentives for tactical voting, by the way the agenda is shaped, and by the sanctions available to party leaders for enforcing party discipline.[34] Comparative research has therefore led to the search for alternative measures of legislators' policy preferences. Cosponsorship of legislation, members' speeches, surveys of members' attitudes, and the positions expressed in party manifestos have been used as alternative indicators of members' preferences in cross-national research.[35]

The measurement problems arising in empirical research on representation are therefore evident on both sides of the link between legislators and their constituents. The challenge lies both in estimating constituents' preferences and legislators' decisions and in making inferences about collective preference from the observations of individuals. However, today we have a much clearer focus on what we are looking for in trying to understand the relationships that constitute the representational properties of legislatures than we did half a century ago, thanks to the attention that the subject has received from political theorists and thanks also to the substantial body of the increasingly comparative empirical research of recent decades.

The ubiquity of legislatures in contemporary political systems worldwide is undoubtedly due to the belief that legislatures are indispensable and irreplaceable political institutions for linking the governed to their governors, even if the linkage varies greatly. The property of representation is therefore one of the two defining characteristics of legislatures, and trying to illuminate this puzzling concept is therefore an inescapable aspect of the study of these bodies. The other puzzling aspect is the formal equality of members of the institution, which arises from their equal status as representatives. These two properties of legislatures, their representativeness and the equality of their members, are directly related. But while representation poses conceptual and empirical puzzles, as we have seen, the formal equality of members poses a range of practical puzzles involving a legislature's organization, its procedure, and its capacity to achieve a collective outcome from the activity of its individual members. This is the subject of the next chapter.

CHAPTER THREE
COLLECTIVE DECISION MAKING

The equal status of each member of a legislature presents a fundamental challenge to its capacity to reach collective decisions. A continuous theme in the history of legislatures over the centuries is how to meet that challenge, which can be simply stated. The authority of a legislature rests on its claim to represent the political community. That claim derives in part from the representativeness of its individual members, each of whom represents a specific part of the community, of a constituency. Every member of a legislature is equally a representative of a constituency and therefore constitutionally equal in status to every other member. That would appear to forbid a hierarchical organization of the institution or any externally imposed efforts to coordinate the actions of members. When we think of other organizations of large numbers of people, say of a corporation, we assume that it will have a leader or a set of leaders, that the individual members will have assigned responsibilities, and that there will be procedures enabling them to achieve specified goals. But the puzzle for legislative organization is how a collection of equals can accept a hierarchy or the imposition of rules to coordinate their actions and how it can ever act without a hierarchy and without rules.

As an additional challenge to legislatures' ability to reach collective decisions, their memberships are hardly ever small. In most countries the sum total of representatives of constituencies produces a very large, unwieldy body. Surprisingly, there is only a weak relationship between the size of a country's population and that of its legislature or between changes in a country's population over time and those in the size of its legislature. Rather, variation in the size of legislatures reflects different concepts of representation implemented by different electoral systems for choosing representatives. For example, the National Assembly of Hungary, elected by a complicated three-tier system of elections, has 386 members for its 10 million citizens, one member for nearly 26,000 people. In the United States, there are 435 members of the House of Representatives for over 300 million people, or one member for over 700,000 people. So, representatives in the United States have twenty-seven times the number of constituents than their Hungarian counterparts. Many European countries—Britain, Germany, and Italy—have legislatures almost 50 percent larger than the United States with only one-fifth the population (see Table 3.1).

Since the size of parliaments has been driven historically by concepts of representation without much regard for how size might affect the capacity to reach collective decisions, there are many anomalies in the relationship between a country's population and the size of its parliament. The Elizabethan House of Commons grew during the sixteenth century from 296 members to 462, twice as quickly as the population.[1] It therefore had more members for 6 million inhabitants in the England of 1700 than the United States has in its House of Representatives today for a population fifty times as large. Some of the new democracies with populations far exceeding those of the older European democracies have parliaments with a smaller number of members. Plotting the relationship shows many outliers (see Figure 3.1). Occasionally legislatures have limited or reduced their size out of a concern for how it affects their capacity to work. The size of the U.S. House of Representatives has been

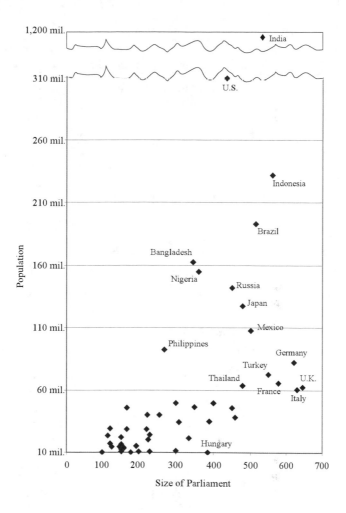

Figure 3.1 Relationship between size of parliament and population
(r = .39)

Table 3.1 Size of Parliament by Population

Country	Population	Size of Parliament	Average Size of Constituency
Hungary	10,013,628	386	25,942
Haiti	10,033,000	99	101,343
Dominican Republic	10,090,000	178	56,685
Czech Republic	10,512,397	200	52,562
Portugal	10,636,888	230	46,247
Belgium	10,827,519	150	72,183
Greece	11,306,183	300	37,687
Senegal	12,534,000	150	83,560
Zambia	12,935,000	158	81,867
Guatemala	14,027,000	158	88,778
Ecuador	14,166,000	124	114,242
Mali	14,517,176	147	98,756
Malawi	15,263,000	193	79,083
Netherlands	16,604,700	150	110,698
Chile	17,062,000	120	142,183
Sri Lanka	20,238,000	225	89,947
Romania	21,466,174	334	64,270
Australia	22,232,000	150	148,213
Taiwan	23,131,093	113	204,700
Ghana	23,837,000	230	103,639
Malaysia	28,306,700	222	127,508
Venezuela	28,746,000	167	172,132
Peru	29,132,013	120	242,767
Canada	34,075,000	308	110,633
Algeria	34,895,000	389	89,704
Poland	38,163,895	460	82,965
Kenya	39,802,000	224	177,688
Argentina	40,134,425	257	156,165
Colombia	45,405,000	166	273,524
Ukraine	45,962,900	450	102,140
Spain	45,989,016	350	131,397
South Africa	49,320,500	400	123,301
Republic of Korea	49,773,145	299	166,465
Italy	60,276,969	630	95,678
United Kingdom	62,041,708	646	96,040

Table 3.1 *(continued)*

Country	Population	Size of Parliament	Average Size of Constituency
Thailand	63,525,062	480	132,344
France	65,447,374	577	113,427
Turkey	72,561,312	550	131,930
Germany	81,757,600	622	131,443
Philippines	92,226,600	269	342,850
Mexico	107,550,697	500	215,101
Japan	127,380,000	480	265,375
Russian Federation	141,927,297	450	315,394
Nigeria	154,729,000	360	429,803
Bangladesh	162,221,000	345	470,206
Brazil	192,806,000	513	375,840
Indonesia	231,369,500	560	413,160
United States of America	309,101,000	435	710,577
India	1,179,787,000	545	2,164,747

kept at a constant 435 members since 1910, regardless of the country's population growth, but similar efforts to limit the size of legislatures in the face of rapid population growth are rare. A century after the U.S. House placed this limit on itself, the average population of its constituencies at over 700,000 is higher than for any other legislature in the world except India. And actually reducing the membership when it is too large is nearly impossible because it requires the votes of the very members who must sacrifice their seats. Two recent instances illustrate the unusual political circumstances that are necessary to make that happen. After the size of the German Bundestag grew from 518 to 656 members after the unification of the two parts of the country, each of which had had its own parliament, the Bundestag voted to reduce its size from 656 to 598 members in the course of other changes made to adapt the political system to unification. And after a single party won an unprecedented two-thirds majority in the Hungarian election of 2010, it imposed a reduction in the size of that exceptionally large parliament by passing a constitutional amendment that did not require the support of any other party. But in both of these instances, unusual circumstances permitted a reduction in a parliament's membership. The conflict between consideration for representativeness and the practical requirements of getting parliamentary work done is just not easy to resolve.

Obviously, whether the membership is relatively small or relatively large, an institution composed of numerous members of equal status cannot act at all unless there is some coordination among them, unless there is at least an agreement on a sequence of decision making and on an agenda. Furthermore, unless there is some agreement on work sharing, some division of labor, many members may try to shirk their duties, to get a "free ride," and will try to avoid making decisions. Agenda setting and division of labor require organization, some constraints on what each member can do, and hence some inequalities among members. The development of organization and procedures for large numbers of members jealous of their equal status has been a matter of institutional learning. Driving institutional learning has been the collective desire of legislatures to have influence in the political system. If they cannot act, then courts, bureaucracies, and monarchs become the decisive actors in the political system. In order to be able to act, legislatures must collectively engage in a trade-off between guarding the equal status of each member and finding ways to coordinate their individual actions. There lies the solution to the organizational puzzle, but it has strange consequences that outsiders have trouble understanding.

The Development of Parliamentary Procedure

There has been a remarkable continuity in legislatures developing appropriate procedures and forms of organization across time and space. Those developments began in the medieval assemblies, which were the antecedents of modern legislatures. The more frequently monarchs convened them, the more these assemblies developed precedents for how they would proceed to consult with the monarch. The development of organization and procedure accelerated in the seventeenth century when the British parliament began to think of itself as a lawmaking body, that is, a body with clear decision-making objectives. Parallel developments occurred in the American colonies as they claimed legislative prerogatives. They had a special incentive for making this claim: It enabled them to assert authority independently of the British Crown. The pragmatic quality of parliamentary procedure is well exemplified by its development in the American colonial legislatures. In his essay tracing of the evolution of U.S. legislatures, Peverill Squire shows that the earliest colonial assemblies imported legislative rules from the British House of Commons. He notes that the speaker of Virginia's House of Burgesses initially made rulings clearly influenced by his earlier service in the House of Commons. But Squire shows that "over time . . . the assemblies adopted increasingly sophisticated rules and procedures of their own devising, significantly different from those used in Parliament."[2] As the colonial assemblies asserted an increasing range of lawmaking powers in the seventeenth and eighteenth centuries, they needed to proceed with ever greater efficiency and developed rules that suited their own needs rather than looking to the British parliament for examples. Squire and Keith Hamm quote the historian S. M. Pargellis, who "marvels at the 'contrast between the few quaint orders of 1663 and the long complete list of 1769.'"[3]

To some extent, the process of institutional learning of effective procedures has been a process of trial and error, with the object always to find ways to reach decisions and avoid paralysis without formally infringing on the equal status of members. The members of the prerevolutionary colonial assemblies in America were aware of these realities. Nearly half of the signers of the U.S. Constitution had served in colonial legislatures. But those who were members of the Continental Congress under the Articles of

Confederation had ignored their previous legislative experience in that setting. In the fluid political situation of Revolutionary America, each member guarded his state's prerogatives jealously and would not accept the kinds of hierarchy that decision making requires. The members of the Continental Congress were unwilling to entrust agenda-setting power to any subset of their members. Consequently, the Congress suffered the disorganization typical of a pure majority-rule institution. One member wrote that he had "been witness to a Report made by a Committee of the Whole, which had been entered upon the Journal, superseded by a new Resolution, even without reference to the Report. [That] Resolution, carried almost [without objection, was] entered [in the Journal] and half an hour [later was] reconsidered and expunged. When I add that such irregularity is the work of almost every day, you will not wonder that I wish to be any where but in Congress."[4]

The Continental Congress also refused to select standing committees to divide the work, relying instead on a huge number of ad hoc committees—more than 3,000 of them were elected between 1774 and 1788—each with little authority and no chance to develop expertise.[5] As a result, most decisions had to be made by all members on the floor of the Congress. Decisions were slow, and the workload of every member was very high. The lineage of American legislatures shows a remarkable continuity from the colonial assemblies, to the legislatures of the states after the Revolution, to the U.S. Congress. But in that lineage, the Continental Congress, under the Articles of Confederation, was what Peverill Squire has called an "evolutionary mutant."[6] Political scientists have loved to study that mutant—the Continental Congress—just as biologists study mutations: to gain insight into normality by examining a failed abnormality.[7]

The process of diffusion tells us something about the complexity of parliamentary procedure and its pragmatic quality. Its principal agents have been parliamentarians and presiding officers, some of whom have compiled the rules that they have applied and the precedents that govern their application. Thus, the long-serving clerk of the British House of Commons from 1768 to 1820, John Hatsell, published the *Precedents of Proceedings in the House of Commons* beginning in 1781, and in 1818 he brought out a four-volume edition, which became the principal source for students of parliamentary procedure throughout the English-speaking world.[8] The similarly influential compilation by Thomas Erskine May, clerk from 1871 to 1886, influenced parliamentary procedure throughout the British Commonwealth.[9] As I mentioned earlier, Thomas Jefferson drew on Hatsell to compile *A Manual of Parliamentary Practice,* which he felt he needed when he presided over the U.S. Senate as vice president of the United States from 1797 to 1801, and Jefferson's *Manual* was eventually incorporated into the rules of procedure of the U.S. House of Representatives. It was also the source of procedure for many of the territorial legislatures that predated state legislatures in many parts of the United States. Parliamentarians of the U.S. House of Representatives, notably Asher C. Hinds, Clarence A. Cannon, and Lewis Deschler, like the clerks of the British House of Commons, have continued to compile the parliamentary precedents governing the work of the U.S. Congress. The German parliament long suffered from the lack of comparable compilations, but in the second half of the twentieth century, its clerks began the process of publishing annotated versions of the rules of the chamber, which constitute the beginnings of a compilation of precedents similar to those that first developed in Great Britain.[10]

Parliaments that do not have a long, continuous history have borrowed their procedures from those that do. The rules of procedure adopted by the German Bundestag in 1951 relied heavily on the rules of the pre-Hitler Reichstag, which in turn was heavily influenced by the rules of the Prussian House of Representatives before German unification. Its rules, in turn, were modeled after those of the British House of Commons, as it was understood on the continent of Europe through the exposition of Jeremy Bentham, whose essay "Parliamentary Tactics,"[11] published in 1816, attempted to describe British procedure in a logical and systematic manner. Bentham's exposition also influenced the French, Belgian, Swiss, and Italian parliaments, although each separate representative body adapted the Benthamite principles to its own evolving needs. These borrowings among European institutions in the nineteenth century had their counterparts among Asian and African legislatures in the twentieth century through diffusion across British and French colonies, facilitated by technical assistance on procedure offered by the British parliament to the assemblies of the British Commonwealth. Technical assistance on procedure from older to newer parliaments was repeated late in the twentieth century with the appearance of newly democratic parliaments in Central and Eastern Europe, many of which looked to the German parliament, which became the model of a legislature that had overcome an authoritarian past. Beginning in 1990, German specialists in parliamentary procedure served as advisers to the parliaments of Hungary, Poland, Slovakia, Slovenia, Estonia, Latvia, Lithuania, Albania, Ukraine, Russia, Bulgaria, Romania, and Macedonia.[12] A nonpartisan, nonnational respect for the complexity of parliamentary procedure explains this pattern of procedural borrowing and makes it possible to trace the procedure of contemporary legislatures ultimately to common medieval European sources.[13]

But there are also limits to the transferability of parliamentary procedures.[14] One example illustrates both the incentives to imitate procedure from one legislature to another and the obstacles to having the transfer take root. The conventional wisdom holds that the U.S. congressional model does not travel well. In form, it seems too rooted in its eighteenth-century origins. In practice, it seems too much shaped by the largesse with which it is staffed and provided with infrastructure. And its political dynamic seems to be the product of an "electoral connection" between its members and their constituents that is the product of a unique political-party system, a system of just two political parties, one of which necessarily commands a majority at any given time, and yet in which the plurality of interests is represented by the internal heterogeneity of each party. All three of these contextual factors affected the attempt of a German legislator to adapt the American "hearings" procedure to the German parliament. He was able to persuade the rules committee of the Bundestag to include a brief provision for hearings in its procedures two years after it first convened. But the procedure was barely used for fifteen years, held in abeyance by the dominance of the executive branch under the leadership of Konrad Adenauer, the first chancellor of the country after World War II. Only after Adenauer's retirement in the mid-1960s, when the balance of power between legislature and executive changed, did legislators have the incentive to use hearings on a considerable scale to gain information and publicize issues, as has been done in the U.S. Congress. Between the adoption of the provision in its rules in 1951 and the retirement of Adenauer, only seven hearings were held under the provisions the Bundestag had copied from the U.S. Congress. But the number climbed rapidly thereafter, and in the twenty-first century, there tend to be about three hundred parliamentary hearings in each legislative term. This recent example of the transfer of a specific legislative procedure from one legislature to another illustrates both the incentive to copy procedures across institutions and the need to take contextual differences into account.[15]

The Elements of Parliamentary Procedure

Legislatures can only manage to make collective decisions by accepting an implicit hierarchy, which entails delegating authority to committees, to party groups, and to leaders. Making collective decisions also entails accepting a set of procedures for reaching those decisions. These hierarchies and procedures inevitably limit the equality of members. Unanimous consent cannot be required for decisions, although some legislatures, notably the U.S. Senate, in fact impose unanimous consent rules on some decisions, creating a severe obstacle to decision making.

The procedures of legislatures cannot even be made consistent with majority rule for reasons that are not intuitively obvious and will require further explanation later in this chapter. The procedures and organizational patterns that legislatures have devised are therefore astonishingly complex and difficult for the casual observer to understand. They are the province of specialists even within legislatures, notably the officials who are called "clerks" in the parliaments with long British traditions or, more aptly, "parliamentarians," which is the title used in U.S. legislatures. These procedures are the product of long experience and are sometimes acquired by veteran lawmakers, who use their mastery of the rules to influence legislative results. As we have seen, important aspects of parliamentary procedure are widely shared among different examples of the institution. Experience over time produces an incredibly large set of rules, reflecting the different constitutional systems in which the world's legislatures exist, their varied functions, and their age. Because legislative procedure has evolved through practice, it consists of rules that have many sources, and the older the legislature, the more diverse the sources. Due to legislatures' insistence on their own autonomy, their rules of procedure are only rarely imposed on them in their national constitution. The attempt by Charles de Gaulle to rein in the French parliament by including procedural restrictions on parliament in the Constitution of 1958 provided a rare example of a legislature constrained in its procedures by the constitution.[16] Half a century later, it was amended as part of a move to restore to some extent the traditional autonomy of parliament in France.[17]

The principal sources of parliamentary procedure are ordinarily the formal rules adopted by the legislature on its own authority and subject to change only by its decisions. But formal rule changes tend to be rare. Since a change of procedure is subject to existing procedure, vested interests in existing procedure present obstacles to change. For example, the rule in the U.S. Senate that permits unlimited debate unless three-fifths of the members adopt a closure resolution cannot be changed by a decision of the majority both because unlimited debate can block consideration of a rules change and because the Senate's procedures prescribe that a change in its rules requires a two-thirds vote. In that sense unlimited debate is entrenched as a minority right in the procedures of the Senate. However, the U.S. Constitution, which has a higher authority than Senate procedure, provides that "each House may determine the Rules of its Proceedings,"[18] which presumably means that the Senate can determine its rules by majority vote. This creates an interesting conflict whose resolution has been instructive. To overcome minority obstruction that Senate procedures appear to entrench, there has occasionally been an appeal to the provisions of the Constitution. However, the formal rules of the Senate and of all legislatures are overlaid with informal understandings that help to avoid deadlock, which a pure application of majority rule on procedures can produce. So, on those rare occasions when there has been an effort to overcome minority rights in the U.S. Senate by a majority vote, that effort has been referred to as the "nuclear option," indicating that members regard it as an extreme violation of informal understandings, to be avoided at almost all costs. Informal understandings and procedures can therefore be even more difficult to change than formal rules and, to the outsider, even more puzzling.

The older the legislature, the more its procedures are embedded in the precedents established in the application of these rules over time, which is why the compilation of precedents is so important as "case law." As I have just shown, procedure is also shaped by informal constraints, customs observed because members find them useful and recognize that they overcome practical problems not readily resolved by majority vote. Examples include reliance on seniority in the naming of committee chairs, still largely followed in the U.S. Congress, the proportional distribution of committee chairs among the political parties in the German Bundestag, and agreement on the length of debates "behind the Speaker's chair" in the British House of Commons.

Finally, in addition to formal rules, precedents, and informal understandings, procedure also consists of the constraints imposed on members by norms of behavior, standards of conduct that prevent the controversies, which are inevitable in legislatures, from becoming disruptive. Thus, legislators who are often profoundly critical of each other's views commonly address each other with exaggerated politeness. To avoid personalizing differences of opinion, members often refer to each other by the constituency they represent: "the Gentlewoman from Maine" or "the Right Honorable Member for Chichester." In most legislatures the presiding officer maintains a code banning personal insults. In the British House of Commons, for example, calling another member a liar, coward, hooligan, rat, traitor, or drunk or accusing another of false motives can lead the Speaker to ask that member to withdraw the comment and, if he refuses, to suspend the member for five days. We can forget that physical violence on the floor of legislatures, rare in long-established parliaments today, was quite common in the earlier history of the institution in Europe and America and keeps coming to the surface in newer legislatures. But we need not look to developing countries today for examples of the propensity of members of legislatures to take out their differences by assaulting each other physically. The legislatures in thirty-one territories organized by the U.S. Congress before these territories were admitted to the Union as states provide hair-raising instances of all kinds of mayhem. Squire relates that

> violence was often resorted to as a way of solving parliamentary problems in territorial legislatures. When a disgruntled group of Dakota House members was unsuccessful in getting the two-thirds vote needed to replace the speaker, they hatched a plan to forcibly unseat him, toss him out a window, and install a new speaker to serve while the old one recovered from his injuries.[19]

The importance of maintaining civility in the face of the controversies endemic to legislatures is not easily learned.

Speakers and Committees

Parliamentary organization and procedure are clearly the complex products of the development of the institution over time and across space. What are the essential aspects of the internal organization of legislatures and the elements of their procedures that make it possible for them to reconcile the equality of their members with a capacity to reach collective decisions? From an early point in their history, parliaments have delegated some power to presiding officers and to committees to organize their work. That is the product of their early experience. When members suffered the cost of discussion without an agenda—as the members of the Continental Congress did—they searched for remedies. Typically they selected a presiding officer. The British parliament appointed a "Speaker" in the fourteenth century to speak to the monarch for the body and later to organize and direct its deliberations. Today, all legislatures elect presiding officers who work together with party-organized steering committees. When members experience the consequence of allowing every member an equal role in every decision, they learn to divide legislative work and to pinpoint responsibility for accomplishing it. Appointing subsets of members as committees, though the typical solution, raises the danger that influence on decisions will be unequal. Not surprisingly, the committee structure of legislatures is the most studied aspect of the organization of contemporary legislatures because it is a principal source of hierarchy within the institution, of authority relationships, and of deference.

Members yield to the authority of committees for three reasons. First, committees provide a division of labor. The resulting specialization permits legislators to develop the information they need to make complex decisions simultaneously on many subjects. Absent committees, legislators would have to depend on interest groups and executive departments for expertise. Deference to committee recommendations is therefore deference to expertise and to efficiency. It can also involve deference to special interests. Second, division of labor among committees provides opportunities for bargaining, enabling members to trade decisions they care little about—decisions made in other committees—for decisions that are crucial to them, decisions in their own committee. Deference to committees protects the bargains struck within a committee from being reopened on the floor of the chamber. And third, committees can be instruments subject to the control of political parties, permitting parties to organize legislative work across subject areas and, in parliamentary systems, between the legislature and the executive. This gives the party-label policy meaning. Members defer to party control because it gives value to the party label, on which their reelection to some extent depends.[20]

For these reasons members who are constitutionally each other's equals have incentives to defer to each other in a variety of ways that permit them to coordinate their work and to obtain results. But the conflict between equality of status and hierarchy never goes away. It leaves the suspicion, among both members and the public, that special interests prevail and that members, though nominally equal to each other, have highly unequal influence on legislative outcomes. The process of appointing committees is therefore very important. In most legislatures the party composition of committees reflects the composition of the parent chamber, but it can also reflect special interests in their area of jurisdiction and may be highly unrepresentative of the chamber as a whole. The low profile of committee decisions and the decentralized decision making they produce facilitate the influence of interest groups, both their legitimate, informational influence and their illegitimate, one-sided influence. Furthermore, the decentralizing effect of a committee system threatens the coherence of the collective decisions of the legislature, notably of its lawmaking and appropriations activity, especially when decisions are referred to several committees simultaneously. The degree of decentralization varies, depending on the number of committees a legislature appoints. The range is very wide, from the low of eight large committees in the French National Assembly to forty-five committees in the Argentine Chamber of Deputies. The U.S. House of Representatives, with twenty standing committees, and the German Bundestag, with twenty-two, fall within the typical range.

But the number of committees is only one aspect of decentralization. The U.S. Congress has carried committee decentralization further than any other legislature because it has an extensive subcommittee structure: In the 111th Congress elected in 2008, the twenty standing committees in the House had 104 subcommittees, and the sixteen standing committees in the Senate had 74 subcommittees. That is a measure of Congress's determination to command the expertise it needs to holds its own against the executive bureaucracy, and it is buttressed by between 30 and 140 staff members for each House committee and between 22 and 153 for each Senate committee. No other legislature comes close to this degree of committee decentralization, to this level of staffing, or indeed to this degree of committee influence on lawmaking and appropriations. In the U.S. House of Representatives, bills are frequently referred to more than one committee. Coordination among them, and between committees in the House and Senate, entails time-consuming negotiation. The relatively small number of French parliamentary committees, and consequently their large membership, is a reaction against the decentralization of decision making that incapacitated the parliaments of France before the de Gaulle constitution of 1958. The British House of Commons has no standing legislative committees at all but appoints a public bill committee separately for each bill under consideration only after it has effectively been approved by a second reading in the whole chamber. That structure, which exists in other parliaments belonging to the British Commonwealth, reflects the cabinet's domination of the legislative process.

The German Bundestag, which has the most highly developed committee system after the U.S. Congress, has twenty-two standing committees, very few of which have subcommittees. However, it also has a highly developed structure of committees within each of the principal political parties in the Bundestag, paralleling the standing committees, and it is in these party committees that the important policy decisions are reached. Each of the two largest parties has between twenty and twenty-two party committees; the smaller ones have four or five. Counting the standing committees and the party committees together, the Bundestag has over eighty legislative committees.[21] So, like the U.S. Congress, the German parliament reflects a high degree of specialization in its committee structure and faces a complex process of coordination, just as Congress does. In the German case, this is a process of both interparty and legislative-executive coordination. And although the standing committees of the German Bundestag do not have large staffs, eight hundred staff members are assigned to the parliamentary parties.

The committee structure to which all legislatures resort permits a division of labor, promotes bargaining that plays on the variation in preference intensities among members across legislative subjects, and above all provides legislatures with some expertise to match the expertise of executive bureaucracies and interest groups. But the committee structure also exacerbates the problem of reaching collective decisions, which involves reconciling the preferences not only of a large number of individuals but of the separate committees into which legislatures divide themselves. Legislatures meet this challenge with a set of procedures that prescribe a decision-making sequence and with decision rules that all members must accept over substantial periods.

Setting the Agenda

We might expect a legislature composed of equals in a democratic setting to proceed in the most egalitarian possible manner, with rules that give no members special powers. That would imply issue-by-issue decisions taken by majority vote. However, there are generally far more issues that individual legislators would like to address than there is time to deal with them, and legislatures must select among them. The extreme example is the Congress of the United States, whose members try to please their constituents by introducing bills without regard to their prospects for passage. Over 10,000 bills have been introduced in recent Congresses, fewer than one-tenth of which have reached enactment. Even if the universe of bills is not in the thousands, all legislatures need agreement on an agenda for choosing among issues and establishing an order for their consideration. That is bound to create inequalities among members, between those who determine the agenda and those who accede to it.

The formal modeling of legislative processes in the last half century has greatly clarified the influence of the agenda on legislative outcomes. William H. Riker, a pioneer in this field of research, summed it up when he wrote that "the process of forming agendas has as much social consequence as individual tastes." He meant that the policy preferences of members of a legislature are not by themselves decisive in determining the outcome of a legislature's deliberations. Instead, the formulation of the agenda of decision making—which subjects are considered when and under what circumstances—may be at least as important in determining outcomes. "As political scientists," Riker wrote, "we ought . . . to study agenda formation just as much as we study political opinion."[22]

In most legislatures, agenda setting was at one time handled via impersonal rules, which sufficed when the number of issues was relatively small. Later, the task was often delegated to a committee of leaders, but in the twentieth century, it increasingly became the province of political parties as they sought to influence legislative decisions. In any case, it requires restrictive procedures because attempting to reach decisions by majority vote is surprisingly likely to lead to deadlock in legislative bodies. This will become clear in the discussion of voting procedures below. In the U.S. House of Representatives, the Rules Committee has wide discretion with regard to agenda setting, including the power to prescribe the sequence of decisions in exact detail. Since the end of the nineteenth century, the Rules Committee has usually been an instrument of the majority party, giving it the ability to advance legislation when it is united or, if it is divided, at least to block legislation.[23] In the U.S. Senate, individual members jealously guard their influence over the agenda, and the majority party leaders have less control. A great deal of the Senate's agenda is set in unanimous consent agreements carefully worked out by the party leaders to take account of the ability of individual senators to block action. In the British House of Commons, the agenda is set within broad guidelines established by customs that have, since the end of the nineteenth century, given the majority party ultimate control but allowed the other parties opportunities to be heard in debate. The details are worked out by the agents of the party leaders, the "whips." So, in both the U.S. House and the British Commons, the majority party controls the agenda, implemented by a small subset of leaders on its behalf. Majority-party control developed in response to minority obstruction when obstruction became increasingly feasible as the number of issues facing legislatures grew.

In continental European parliaments in which no party has a majority, interparty agenda negotiations reflect the distribution of power among the parties in the legislature. There is therefore an important difference between a two-party system that gives the governing majority party control of the parliamentary agenda and a multiparty system that requires broad agenda agreement among a coalition of parties. Attempting to set the agenda by majority vote is likely to result in deadlock, so the parties seek consensus. To reinforce interparty agreements, restrictive procedures, formal or informal, are usually employed to maintain the agreements that the parties negotiate. In the German Bundestag the agenda is effectively managed by the whips appointed by the political parties in parliament, who have a managerial interest in maintaining their control, which their party followers do not challenge.[24] In the French National Assembly, the agenda is negotiated between the government and the parliamentary parties, and agreement is supported by restrictive procedures provided in the constitution.[25] Consensus among the parties on the agenda is sought in both Germany and France. In Italy, however, where there has generally been a sharper division between government and opposition, the governing coalition has been able to set the agenda without serious challenge from the opposition parties.[26] For practical reasons, based on long experience, restrictive procedures, whether provided in written rules or informally arranged, have great staying power.

In Latin America, where presidential systems modeled after the American system give presidents greater power, legislatures are best described as "reactive."[27] As an indicator of executive dominance in these legislatures, the agenda is effectively set by the president, because the president has the power to introduce legislation and, in many countries, to impose an urgency procedure that compels legislatures to give presidential bills priority.[28]

The Party Organization of Legislatures

The study of agenda formation and committee organization reveals the extent to which political parties shape the aggregation of individual member's preferences in a modern parliament. That development is the result of the democratization of parliaments because parties arose in response to the need to organize an expanded electorate. To be sure, there were parties in parliament before the advent of democracy. James Madison railed against the "mischiefs of faction,"[29] but these groupings within parliaments were not connected to the voters on the outside until democratization created ever larger electorates. In the United States this development came in the 1820s. In continental European parliaments, it first appeared in the revolutions of 1848. Parties can be detected in the analysis of votes in the French Constituent Assembly and the Frankfurt Assembly in Germany in that year.[30] Then "party" became an important organizational structure within parliament as well as a valuable label for candidates. The value of the label began to depend on its meaning for policy.

The differences between individual legislators' own policy preferences and those of their party are resolved differently at different times and in different countries, depending in part on differences in electoral systems. But wherever party influence is felt in the organization and procedure of legislatures, it contributes to the possibility of collective action. Without party organization in contemporary legislatures, collective action would be either difficult to achieve or the product of interest groups and of other influences not accountable to the electorate. Political parties provide solutions to the collective-action dilemmas that face legislators acting alone: how to coordinate their activities within the legislature to get the best possible results for every member and how to develop reputations translatable into electoral appeal. Political parties are therefore critically important organizations in nearly all democratic legislatures, influencing the appointment of committees and determining the agenda of both committees and the legislature as a whole. The smallest state legislature in the United States, the forty-nine-member Nebraska Unicameral, is the conspicuous exception to the prevalence of party organization in legislatures, but its small size enables it to find substitutes for party organization. Nostalgia for the independent member acting only according to the dictates of his or her conscience is nostalgia for a predemocratic political system and reflects a naive view of how an assembly can best serve the general welfare. The sum of the goals of individual legislators leaves out of account goals that can only be achieved by cooperation, goals that take the form of public goods that cannot be subdivided. This is exemplified very clearly today by concern for the global environment, which is threatened by the sum total of the wishes of individual legislators serving their individual constituencies.

Party influence varies, depending on the cohesiveness of parties, the degree of their centralization, and their number. In the United States, the federal structure of government and the single-member-constituency system of elections have counterbalanced party centralization and party cohesion. But beginning in the last third of the twentieth century, a regional realignment of attitudes toward the principal political issues in the country produced politically homogeneous geographic regions dominated by one party or the other. This greatly increased party cohesion in Congress, to a level comparable to the general cohesiveness of European and Latin American political parties. The ideological and class basis of parties in the countries on those continents, especially on the political right and left, had always made these parties highly disciplined organizations. On the other hand, the multiplicity of political parties outside the United States makes their influence on legislative decisions dependent on the formation of coalitions in the legislature or in the cabinet. This creates the need for methods of interparty coordination that include coalition committees and coalition treaties, which have only recently become subjects of legislative research.[31] It is symptomatic of the importance of political parties in legislatures that where only a single party exists, the legislature is deprived of independent influence in the political system.

Voting Procedures

That one cannot rely on majority rule to make decisions in legislatures seems strange. It would seem obvious that decisions in a democratic institution would be made by majority vote. Just why this is usually not possible is another puzzle to outsiders. The puzzle can be understood by recognizing that, unlike voters in general elections, legislators vote on a constant stream of issues, and as they do, they interact with each other and endeavor to negotiate compromises. Instead of voting up or down on separate issues, they develop multiple alternatives. When an individual legislator votes among these alternatives, he or she may have rational, and what are called transitive, preferences among them. Preferences are said to be transitive if preferring the first alternative to the second and the second to the third also means preferring the first to the third. A single legislator with transitive preferences can therefore choose decisively among alternatives in a sequence of votes. But one legislator may well have a different order of preferences from another. Therefore, in successive votes among pairs of alternatives, there will likely be not one majority but many, each comprising different individuals.

Choosing among alternatives in a legislature can therefore result in an endless cycle of votes, each producing a majority. If one stops the cycle at an arbitrary point and declares a winner, the particular sequence of votes among these alternatives, if they are paired against each other, decides the outcome. When the preferences of individual legislators are aggregated for a group of legislators, a single decisive majority outcome is very unlikely. This means that the collective preferences of a group are not usually transitive, even if every individual member of the group does have his or her own transitive preferences. When a group of legislators is likely to contain many majorities, rather than just one, on a set of alternative choices, there is just no way of choosing among them by majority vote.

An example can make that clear. Let us say that a legislature faces a decision about whether to raise income, corporation, or sales taxes. It can easily happen, in successive votes between two alternatives at a time, that the sales tax will defeat the income tax, the corporation tax will defeat the sales tax, and the income tax will defeat the corporation tax. But from the earlier pairing, we know that the income tax will be defeated by the sales tax, so if voting continues, the preference cycle will begin again, unless there is some rule to stop it. Often there is no single majority but several majorities, each composed of different legislators, and a nonmajoritarian rule is needed to reach a decision. Each legislator may have his or her own, perfectly consistent set of preferences. But the sum of those preferences will be inconsistent and unstable. We have what are called cycling majorities.

The possibility of votes leading to cycling majorities has long been recognized: It was clearly articulated at the end of the eighteenth century by the French philosopher, legislator, and mathematician the Marquis de Condorcet,[32] and it forms the basis of the theorem for which Kenneth Arrow won a Nobel Prize in economics.[33] Arrow's theorem demonstrates that there is no way to translate the rational preferences of individuals between pairs of alternatives into the coherent, consistent, stable preferences of a group, except by imposing nonmajoritarian rules on the voting procedure. Legislatures commonly do that by imposing a particular sequence on voting or by restricting the right of amendment.

In the British parliament and most English-speaking legislatures, including the U.S. Congress, an amendment procedure is used by which pairs of alternatives are compared, and one is removed at each voting stage.[34] Of course, voting need not be organized as choices between pairs of alternatives. In many European legislatures, alternatives are voted on one by one in succession instead of in pairs, and the voting stops as soon as one alternative receives a majority. In this procedure the importance of the sequence by which alternatives are presented for vote is even more clearly evident than it is in paired votes. Legislatures that employ this procedure, recognizing the importance of sequence, usually follow the principle that the most extreme alternative is voted on first, on the assumption that if it fails, less extreme alternatives should be considered in succession until one is reached that commands adequate support. This requires an objective judgment about the relative degree of change entailed in each alternative. Whether voting is by pairs of alternatives or in a succession of proposals, the sequence in which votes are taken strongly influences the outcome.

Experienced legislators, who often acquire great skill in exploiting particular sequences to their own advantage, have always recognized the importance of sequence. They have attempted to influence results by engaging in "tactical" voting, that is, voting with an eye to an eventual result rather than as an expression of their sincere preferences at each stage. The ordinary citizen, watching the voting process in the legislature, is bound to view it cynically. Naively, citizens expect that it should be simple to aggregate the decisions of individuals into the decisions of a group. But it is not simple at all and creates a conflict between the idea of majority rule and the reality of decision making in large bodies.

Bicameralism

Committee organization, party organization, and procedural constraints all seem in principle to conflict with the equal status of every member of a representative legislature, and all seem to contribute to the ordinary citizen's mistrust of the institution. Fully two-fifths of the world's legislatures exhibit one other characteristic that seems to conflict with the equal status of members: their division into two chambers. Bicameralism, another product of the medieval origin of representative assemblies, originally expressed social-class differences, the need for the separate accommodation of representatives of the nobility. In the subsequent history of the institution, new rationales developed for a bicameral structure. In colonial America bicameralism was the result of the need to distinguish between the appointees of the British Crown, who eventually sat separately, from the indigenously chosen representatives of the colonists. Bicameralism in America preceded the establishment of a federal system of government, which later became the justification for two very differently composed chambers. Federalism is today the principal justification for having two chambers at the national level, but many unitary states have bicameral legislatures, some to give special representation to regions or ethnic groups, some merely to express different conceptions of representation. In two-thirds of the second chambers, the members are either indirectly elected or appointed. Reflecting the continuity of the development of legislatures in the United States, forty-nine of its fifty state legislatures are also bicameral. The reconciliation between the decisions of two chambers adds a procedural complexity to the legislative process that has been extensively analyzed in the last twenty years by conceptualizing the two chambers as "veto players" engaged in a competitive game whose outcome depends on their respective constitutional powers, the policy preferences of their members, their internal rules of procedure, their "patience" with each other, and the rules and mechanisms for achieving agreement between them.[35] In many bicameral systems, a special committee exists to reconcile differences between the decisions of the two chambers, and the strategic position of such a committee as the last actor in the legislative process gives it exceptional influence. That has been demonstrated in research on the Conference Committee in the United States.[36] In Germany, a similar committee composed of an equal number of members of each legislative chamber has a different consequence. The second chamber in Germany, the Bundesrat, is not directly elected like the U.S. Senate but reflects the party composition of the sixteen state governments, each of which appoints members to represent it. The decisions of this committee therefore reflect the differences, sometimes quite pronounced, between the party coalition that has a majority in the national parliament and the sum of the party coalitions that rule in the states.[37] These differences can produce gridlock in the legislative process, the German counterpart to the gridlock that can exist in the United States when the presidency and the Congress are in the hands of different parties.

While bicameralism originated in the class structure that existed at the time of the medieval origins of parliaments, its remarkable survival expresses the ambiguity of the concept of representation and its various manifestations in different countries. In the United States it preserves a concept of representation of states as components of a federal system and creates extreme disproportion in the ratio of representatives to population between voters in the smallest state, Wyoming, and the largest state, California. This constitutes a disproportion of seventy to one in the ratio of population to senators, the third largest ratio of disproportionality in the world. But it is so entrenched in the U.S. Constitution that it is impossible to change, even if a major reform of representation were to attract wide public support.[38] Likewise in Germany, bicameralism expresses a concept of representation of the states (*Länder*) that preceded German national unification in 1871 and again preceded the establishment of the Federal Republic in 1949. While it does not create as great a disproportion in the ratio of representatives to population as the Senate does in the United States, the Bundesrat, composed of appointees of the state governments, is an unelected body with power equal to that of the elected chamber on a constitutionally specified set of bills that make up almost half of all legislation.

In these ways bicameralism sustains a pre- or nondemocratic concept of representation, but one that, particularly in federal systems, continues to find strong support. Indeed, bicameralism assists the development and survival of multinational, multiethnic, federal systems and finds a new application in supranational communities like the European Union. Where it exists, it divides legislators into two groups of sometimes equal, but often highly unequal, status and adds inertia to the decision-making process. Although some countries have abolished their second legislative chambers in the last half century, there are often constitutional or political obstacles to such "rationalization" or "modernization." The century-long effort to reform or abolish the British House of Lords, which is most clearly descended from a medieval conception of representation, shows the tenacity of bicameralism as a feature of the legislative institution. Taking bicameralism as only one aspect of the system of veto players, George Tsebelis has developed a general theory of the effect of political institutions on policy outcomes. He concludes that the more veto players of all kinds there are in a political system, the less the executive branch controls the political agenda and the more influential the legislature tends to be. In turn, this reduces the capacity of the political system to bring about policy change.[39] From this perspective bicameralism affects the role of the legislature in the political system far more extensively than is generally realized.

At the outset I referred to the genetic properties of legislatures present in them from the beginning: they are a collection of influential people, they represent others, and they bargain with the government on behalf of their constituents. The institution has survived the inherent contradictions that arise from these properties by puzzling and often misunderstood adaptations. The proud and influential members of legislatures have had to accept constraints on the equality of each other's status. These constraints have been imposed by complex and counterintuitive procedures, sometimes formally written down but more often informally transmitted, and by hierarchies, sometimes visible, often implicit, and usually hard to challenge. More than any other political institution, legislatures are open to the public. Its members want to reach out to their constituents, some of whom in turn want to make contact with their representatives. But casual acquaintance with legislators and the legislature makes the incongruities between its generic properties and necessary adaptations puzzling or, often enough, maddening. Effective communication between legislatures and the public is a basic challenge, to which I turn in the next chapter.

CHAPTER FOUR
LEGISLATURES AS LINKS
BETWEEN GOVERNMENT
AND THE PUBLIC

Although parliaments existed centuries before the advent of democracy and nation states, elected parliaments are today a defining characteristic of democracy and national independence. The association between parliaments, democracy, and national independence explains the remarkable proliferation of this originally medieval institution in the modern world. In its many manifestations, the legislature has developed distinctively different roles in the varied political systems in which it exists. As we have seen, legislatures were originally a purely consultative institution. Then, beginning in the seventeenth century, they became the instruments by which the American colonies asserted their authority independently of the British Crown, a process repeated later in Latin America and then in the British and French empires. Parliaments in these cases were instruments of nation building and, by asserting lawmaking authority, they also became participants in the process of governance. In nineteenth-century Europe, elected parliaments were the instruments by which monarchical regimes were democratized, so the association of parliaments with democratization begins there. By the

twentieth century, legislatures had become a symbol of the legitimacy of regimes to such an extent that even the most
stringently authoritarian governments, such as those of the Soviet Union, the Communist states of Eastern Europe, and the
Middle Eastern monarchies, used legislatures as window dressing. In the second half of the twentieth century, the
multiplication of independent states produced a large number of
new legislatures. Approximately three-quarters of the legislatures
in the world today were established after 1945. Everywhere they
were symbols of nation building. In some instances—but by no
means in all—they also assumed significant governmental functions. No self-respecting regime today is without a legislature.
The institution is ubiquitous, everywhere indispensable in providing a link between government and the public.

The Electoral Connection of Legislators

On the face of it, legislatures should be popular, but one of the
enduring puzzles is that they are not. They should be able to
give the public influence over government. They have closer ties
to the public than do bureaucratic or judicial institutions. They
are designed to provide avenues for public contact with government. And they presume to represent the public. Although
representation had other meanings earlier in the history of legislatures—in status societies, representatives could be appointed,
choose themselves, or inherit their representative positions, as
did the members of the British House of Lords—in the modern
world election by constituencies through one means of voting
or another is the indispensable condition of representativeness.
That process is imitated even in countries that we would not
regard as democratic. The implication of the electoral connection is that legislators have an incentive to serve their
constituents, to elicit their support, and to maintain close ties.

Indeed, in many countries, particularly those in which legislators represent single-member constituencies, the individual

representative appears to be popular among members of the attentive public. But a question not often asked is how visible the individual representative really is to the mass electorate. In one of the few truly comparative studies of the visibility of legislative candidates in France and the United States, Philip E. Converse and Roy Pierce concluded that candidate visibility varies greatly with the institutional context of elections, the number of candidates for each seat (a relatively high number in a multiparty system), the number of offices to be filled (a relatively high number in the U.S. two-party system), and the turnout for elections (relatively low for midyear congressional elections in the United States). The authors of this study also found that incumbent candidates in the United States strongly believed that their reelection resulted from their personal standing, and French incumbents believed it was due to their party label.[1] Earlier research had suggested that winning candidates in elections believed that their victory was due to their personal records, while losing candidates believed their defeat was due to factors outside their control.[2] This "congratulation-rationalization effect" encouraged legislators to place an emphasis on pleasing their constituents. While that emphasis may well vary with the institutional context of elections, as Converse and Pierce suggested, what matters for the behavior of legislators is that they believe everywhere in the importance of serving their constituents.

The strong inclination that members feel to maintain their individual popularity leads them to put effort into constituency service. Minimally this takes the form of doing "errands" for constituents, obtaining information, contacting executive departments, and giving advice. The ability of members to do such favors depends in part on whether they have staff assistance, which varies enormously from one country to another. Members of the U.S. Congress have offices both in Washington and in their districts, and these offices constitute veritable enterprises, with staffs averaging fifteen individuals for House members and forty for senators. In most other countries, members' personal staffs are tiny by comparison or do not exist at all.

Members of the British House of Commons and of the German Bundestag have personal staffs of three to four individuals each, a typical size for members' personal offices where they exist. Service to constituents is the most widespread activity in which members of legislatures are engaged worldwide, even when they do not represent individual constituencies but are elected in multimember districts. Members hold office hours in their constituencies, communicate by telephone and mail, participate in community activities, and are active in the party organization of their constituencies. In developing countries, notably in most of Africa, where members of parliament have little ability to do anything beyond this kind of service, the result has been to maintain a "patron-client" relationship between members and their constituencies, helping to preserve a patrimonial political system.[3] In Germany, where a mixed proportional and single-member electoral system exists, half of all members—and nearly all members of smaller parties—gain their seats in multimember constituencies. Nevertheless, each member "adopts" a single-member constituency to serve, even if not elected by one. In all electoral systems and party systems, members have a strong incentive to respond to their constituents with service. So, constituency service is one potential source of the popularity of the individual representative.

A more significant source of individual members' popularity is their ability to provide public goods to their constituencies, which depends on the role of individual members in the appropriations process. While in most countries this is dominated by the executive branch, in many countries it is heavily influenced by interest groups and political parties. In the United States appropriations are substantially shaped by the decisions of the appropriations and budget committees of each chamber. This encourages a pattern of distributive politics by which members trade favors with each other for their respective constituencies, disregarding the cumulative cost imposed on the national budget. Richard F. Fenno Jr.'s previously quoted observation that "we love our congressmen so much more than our Congress" can be explained by the fact that voters evaluate their representatives primarily by their constituency service and by the "pork" they bring home, by the appropriations they "earmark" for their districts, not by their policy positions or their general competence. In this respect the members of the U.S. Congress have the greatest capacity to ingratiate themselves with their constituencies of any legislators elsewhere in the world. In other legislatures, parties or party factions can ingratiate themselves in this way. However, as we have seen, the popularity of the individual member or a party group in the legislature, whether in developed or developing countries, does not translate into popularity for the legislative institution as a whole.

In the United States, members of Congress often run for reelection by running against Congress, claiming credit for everything they have done for their constituency and blaming their colleagues for everything that the public regards as wrong with the institution. In other countries, especially where parties occupy distinct policy positions within the legislature, members run for reelection by running against members of the other parties. By criticizing the members of rival parties, they obliquely disparage the institution by claiming that it enables these parties to delay decisions, block needed action, or enact measures having little public support. This was strikingly illustrated in the U.S. congressional election of 2010, when the Republicans asserted that only the peculiarities of the legislative process in Congress permitted the Democrats to win passage of U.S. health reform legislation, which the American public, Republicans charged, strongly opposed. The paradoxical pattern of running for reelection to the legislature by running against the legislature itself is widespread.

The disjunction between evaluations of parliament as a whole and citizens' evaluation of their own member may also be a special case of the perceptual bias that exists between evaluations of people who are close and familiar and those who are distant and "other."[4] So, public criticism of Congress or the House of Commons or the Bundestag or the Kenyan National

Assembly can exist side by side with each constituency's approval of its own member. This is exacerbated by legislators' tendency to ingratiate themselves with their constituents via services and public goods while criticizing the institution to which they belong. In this way they use incumbency as a ticket to repeated reelection while undercutting the institution to which they are individually eager to belong. These are the reasons why the electoral bonds between voters and their representatives fail to make elected legislatures popular.

The Capacity of Legislatures to Control the Actions of the Executive

Legislatures have been the chosen instruments of democratization because giving their members the power to make laws presumably gives them the capacity to control the executive branch of the government. But the control of government in the modern world entails more than establishing the legal norms that organize and circumscribe governmental action. It entails regulation of governmental expenditures and appointments, oversight over government decisions, and control over the discretion of the bureaucracy. The capacity of legislatures to exercise these controls varies greatly. Analysis of that capacity has used a "principal-agent" concept, which I mentioned in chapter 2 in the discussion of representation; in the present case, the legislature is regarded as the "principal" in this relationship and the bureaucracy as its "agent." A cross-national analysis using this concept demonstrates that there is great institutional variation in the capacity of legislatures to control the government. All other things being equal, the legislature's control can be greater in presidential systems, in which the legislature is separate from the executive, than in parliamentary systems. In presidential systems legislatures can formulate detailed laws to limit bureaucratic discretion effectively. Their ability to do that depends on the level of professionalization of the legislature, its staffing levels, and the stability of its membership over time. In parliamentary systems, especially when party discipline is high and the cabinet enjoys the support of a majority party in parliament, executive auton omy is likely to be great, both because ministers who sit in parliament exercise extensive influence over the content of legislation and because they also influence its implementation. But in parliamentary systems in which government consists of a coalition of parties, legislative control is similar to that which exists in presidential systems. Furthermore, where cabinets stay in office for relatively short durations—where parliamentary systems exhibit cabinet instability—legislative control does not effectively limit the bureaucracy.[5]

The influence of legislatures over appointments, appropriations, and oversight also varies greatly. The power of the U.S. Senate to confirm approximately 1,000 presidential appointments has no counterpart elsewhere and has assumed greater importance as the Senate has made increasing use of the right of a two-fifths minority to block consideration of appointments. That right has morphed into the ability of single senators to place a "hold" on the confirmation of appointments, a reflection of the need for unanimous agreement on agenda decisions. As a result, a new administration is often unable to fill administrative positions for many months after coming to office. Although the power to confirm appointments is specific to the U.S. Senate, other legislatures often act as the electorate for filling government positions. In twenty-five European countries, parliaments elect, or participate in the election of, the holders of five important offices: the head of state, the members of the constitutional court, the chair of the central bank, the head of the national audit office, and the ombudsperson. In this way parliaments exercise influence over how these important positions are filled, but there is little evidence that they enable parliaments to exercise control over the actions of the holders of these offices.[6] The most important way that legislatures influence the composition of the executive branch is in the process of forming cabinets in the parliamentary system, which I will discuss below.

In giving legislatures control over the government, their right to appropriate funds and determine the government's budget was one of the most insistent claims of the American colonists, based on the traditional right of the British parliament to raise revenues and appropriate funds. "No taxation without representation" was the slogan repeatedly used by the colonists in the decade before the Revolution since they were denied representation in the British House of Commons. Because of this history, the power to tax and spend is one of the most significant powers of the U.S. Congress. However, most parliamentary systems follow the principle established in the British parliament in the eighteenth century that financial measures can only be introduced in parliament by a member of the cabinet, in Britain by ministers on behalf of the Crown. In most parliamentary systems, therefore, the initiative to propose the budget, raise taxes, and appropriate funds is reserved to the executive, usually by constitutional provisions.

The effectiveness of legislative oversight depends on the extensiveness of the committee system. The incentive to exercise oversight is stronger under a separation-of-powers system than in a parliamentary system. As I have shown, the adoption of a hearings procedure, American style, by the German parliament serves as an example of procedural borrowing from a presidential into a parliamentary system whose success depended on the development of a balance of power between legislature and executive in the adopting country.

How legislatures exercise control over the executive branch of the government on behalf of the public they represent depends on their influence over legislation, appointments, appropriations, and oversight. Their influence therefore varies across both constitutional and party systems. The mere existence of a popularly elected legislature by no means assures the effectiveness of that control; nor is it necessarily a source of public support for this instrument of democratization.

The Capacity of Legislatures to Control the Composition of the Executive in Parliamentary Systems

In parliamentary systems, the legislature's most important means of controlling the executive is by its role in the formation and dismissal of the cabinet, which leads the executive branch and is customarily called "the government." In the traditional parliamentary system only the legislature is directly elected; the executive is not. But the composition of the executive reflects the composition of the legislature. In their carefully worked-out model of the cabinet-formation process, Michael Laver and Kenneth Shepsle wrote, "Governments in parliamentary democracies are created by legislators and may be destroyed by them. But, while they are in existence . . . legislatures have only very limited control over the precise policy outputs governments enact."[7] In parliamentary systems, therefore, legislatures achieve their policy aims principally by influencing the composition of the cabinet, based on the existing distribution of seats among the parties in parliament or on the result of a redistribution of seats after an election. Among the possible cabinet compositions that can command the requisite support of a majority in parliament at any moment, Laver and Shepsle analyzed the factors that make a cabinet strong and durable. They demonstrate that the strongest cabinet is one in which each ministerial position is assigned to the party among those making up a parliamentary majority that holds the median position on the policy in that ministry's jurisdiction.[8] In that way the composition of the cabinet reflects the party composition of the parliament, which is in turn the product of an election.

The stability of such a cabinet is undermined if members do not observe party discipline in voting, but for this reason party discipline tends to be high in parliamentary systems. In the absence of discipline, parties cannot achieve their policy goals. Party leaders can command the discipline of their followers by controlling members' advancement toward cabinet positions. Leaders can also exert discipline by influencing their followers' renomination.[9] But the stability of a cabinet can also be under-mined by external events. In the typical parliamentary system, elections do not necessarily come at fixed times but may result from a dissolution of parliament before its term expires. This may occur when political leaders who are constitutionally enti-tled to dissolve parliament expect that a new election will result in a redistribution of seats in their favor, an expectation not always realized in the outcome of the election that follows.

The public holds the legislature responsible for cabinet sta-bility in parliamentary systems. In the last forty years, there has been a great deal of research into factors that affect that stabili-ty. Conclusions distinguish between the effect of the composition of cabinets, which reflects the composition of the legislature, and the impact of external events, which reflect the vulnerability of the legislature to new elections.[10]

Cabinet instability in many continental European democra-cies in the time between the two world wars contributed substantially to public approval of the suspension of parliaments and support for strong executives and authoritarian rule. A pathol-ogy developed in the parliamentary systems of Germany, Italy, Hungary, Poland, and Spain as economic crises strengthened rad-ical political parties and made the formation of stable cabinet coalitions difficult and eventually impossible. Benito Mussolini's "march on Rome" in 1922 and Adolf Hitler's election successes a decade later led to their appointment as prime minister and chan-cellor, respectively, and once in office they effectively suspended parliament, encountering no organized public opposition. Parlia-ment was displaced in Poland by a military coup d'état in 1926, and in the years leading to World War II, parliaments were pushed aside in Bulgaria, Hungary, Romania, and Spain.

The desire to overcome cabinet instability in the post–World War II period brought constitutional innovations that reduced the influence of parliaments on the formation of cabinets in various ways. One approach was a constitutional stip-ulation that parliament could not vote a cabinet out of office without replacing it with another. The requirement of a "constructive no-confidence vote," limiting parliament's power to overthrow cabinets, was first provided in the German Basic Law in 1949 and forty years later in several Eastern European states. A second approach was to combine a presidential system with a parliamentary system. This type of semipresidential government, first established in France in 1958, was later imitated in Poland and elsewhere in Eastern Europe, in some post-Soviet states, and in some African countries. It creates some ambiguity as to the relative power of the prime minister, who is responsible to parliament, and the president, who is popularly elected. That constitutional ambiguity creates particular tension when the president belongs to a different party from the parties having a majority in parliament, to whom the prime minister is responsible. It places the initiative for the appointment and dismissal of the prime minister into the hands of the president but does not necessarily enable the president to control the prime minister's actions. The tendency has been to leave the president with authority in foreign policy, which can be conducted without extensive parliamentary support, and to require consensus between president and prime minister on domestic policy. Finally, provisions were put into many constitutions to limit the possibility of calling elections before the end of a parliament's constitutional term. The result is that cabinet stability has been greater in Europe in the last half century than it was between the two world wars, and public acceptance of parliament is certainly stronger. Paradoxically, popular support for parliaments has been achieved at the expense of parliament's influence over the formation and dismissal of cabinets.

Although cabinet stability is greater now than before 1945, the formation of cabinets remains a time-consuming process of negotiation unless a single party can command a majority, which is usually, but not always, the case in Great Britain, or when the costs of reconstituting a coalition are low because the number of possible coalitions is very limited.[11] Everywhere else, interparty negotiation, which often results in an elaborate coalition treaty spelling out the policy agreements, generates public impatience with parliament. This impatience grows with each passing week of negotiation and leads to criticism of the whole system if the resulting coalition fails before the end of the parliamentary term.

Comparing Popular Influence over Government in Presidential and Parliamentary Systems

The principal institutional alternative to the democratization of government by legislatures has been democratization by the direct election of the head of government. A move in that direction was first taken, hesitantly, by the writers of the U.S. Constitution at the end of the eighteenth century. The framers devised a complicated electoral college as an intermediary between the electorate and the choice of the president. The development of political parties almost immediately thereafter provided the growing electorate with considerable influence over the selection of the president, though it remained—and remains—something short of direct election. In the course of the nineteenth and twentieth centuries, direct election was adopted in the presidential systems of Latin America, was superimposed on a parliamentary system in the German constitution of 1919, and was adopted in some Asian and African countries after they gained independence, as well as in many post-Soviet states after the collapse of the Communist regimes. But as I have shown above, legislatures can influence the actions of the government in presidential systems without having a hand in the selection of the head of the government. In parliamentary systems, legislatures influence the government by the role they play in the composition and stability of the cabinet. Assessing which is the more democratic arrangement, a presidential or a parliamentary system, together with the contextual factors that determine this—the electoral system and the party configuration—became an important research subject during the third wave of democratization at the end of the twentieth century.[12]

The susceptibility of presidential systems to presidential dictatorship in many settings led to two new arrangements of legislative influence over government in several presidential systems in the second half of the twentieth century. The first involved the hybrid semipresidential systems mentioned earlier. While presidents are directly elected in such systems, executive power is shared with a prime minister and a cabinet responsible to parliament. The relative powers of president and prime minister in this dual executive, as well as the party affiliation of each, determine whether they act as a united executive or "cohabit," as the French say.[13] Under "cohabitation," parliament is an important linking mechanism. The second new arrangement in presidential systems developed in the consolidation of democracy in Latin America at the end of the twentieth century. That consolidation strengthened the ability of Latin American legislatures to constrain the traditionally dominant presidents. While Latin American legislatures do not exercise significant policy-making initiatives in these systems—they have been characterized as "reactive" rather than "proactive"—legislative and executive powers are so arranged that presidents must anticipate the legislature's policy positions in exercising their policy-making powers. The presidents' legislative initiative in Latin America, combined with the existence of multiparty systems, makes coalition cabinets indispensable, and the formation and support of these coalitions involve parliament. Having cabinet ministers hold seats in the legislature—precluded by the constitution in the United States—also gives the presidential system in Latin America some of the characteristics of European parliamentary systems, though there is great variation among them.[14] At the beginning of the twenty-first century, about half of the world's democracies were parliamentary, the same proportion as half a century earlier, but of the remaining half, one-third were of the new hybrid kind.[15]

While the president is directly elected in the new hybrid presidential systems in Europe and Latin America, both of these systems give the legislature considerable influence over the executive. Fear of presidential dictatorship motivates the effort to keep the legislature in the loop between government and public. The German experience with presidential dictatorship in the Weimar Republic, earlier French experience with Bonapartism, and Latin American experience with presidential dictatorship explain the efforts to create constitutional systems that combine the characteristics of presidential and parliamentary systems. But while the combination has not necessarily made legislatures popular, it has not undermined them in the way parliaments were undermined in Europe between 1920 and 1940, when they were regarded as the source of executive weakness. Meanwhile, the propensity of pure presidential systems toward dictatorship remains evident in many African, Middle Eastern, post-Soviet, and Asian political systems. In the twenty-first century, legislatures continue to be a bulwark of democracy.

Estimating Public Support for Legislatures

Although historically, and by constitutional design, legislatures are supposed to link government to the public, I have noted in several contexts that legislatures are puzzlingly unpopular. But it is also true that it is difficult to measure the level of public support for legislatures reliably at any given moment or over time. The institution in the abstract attracts a positive valence in the United States and in many democratic countries, even where an elected legislature is new. However, the legislature as a collection of politicians usually elicits negative public attitudes. This means that it is difficult to measure public attitudes toward legislatures in all of their dimensions and to compare these attitudes with those toward other political—and nonpolitical—institutions. Where legislatures are engaged in lawmaking or, more generally, in policy making, it is difficult to disentangle public attitudes to the institution of the legislature from those toward its policy decisions—or indecisions. Survey research in the United States has used various questions to tap attitudes toward Congress, referring to "trust," "respect," and "support" for the institution and to "confidence" in it. It is not clear whether question wording makes a difference in the result.[16] The longest time series, provided by the Gallup Poll, asks respondents whether they "approve or disapprove of the way Congress is handling its job." Support for Congress, no matter how measured, is lower than support for the other principal institutions of government, but it is not static. Variance over time is related to general political conditions in the country and to the particular issues confronting Congress at a given moment. For example, approval of Congress peaked at 54 percent after the 9/11 attack on the United States in 2001—a familiar "rally 'round the flag" reaction. It reached a low of 14 percent in 2008 as the economy went into a severe recession.[17] There are also sharp partisan differences in public evaluations. Democrats evaluate a Democratically controlled Congress more favorably than Republicans, and vice versa. In a conflict between president and Congress, Congress is most often viewed negatively as a cause of "gridlock."[18] In short, what is most visible about Congress—its lawmaking activity or inactivity—drives public attitudes toward it as an institution, and this is true in other countries as well as in the United States.

To the extent that survey research measures the popularity of parliaments and legislatures according to public trust in the institution as a whole, popularity is low both in absolute terms and relative to other governmental institutions in most established democracies. Moreover, it has been declining for the past generation. The army, the police, the courts, and the legal system generally attract the highest levels of trust.[19] Trust in the administration of government tends to be higher than trust in parliaments and parties, which are generally trusted least.[20] The same pattern evident in long-established democracies holds true for Germany, where an exceptional effort was made to establish a strong parliament sixty years ago after the catastrophe that followed the collapse of parliamentary government in the 1930s,[21] as well as for the post-Communist countries of Central and Eastern Europe, where competitively elected parliaments have existed for less than one generation but were established in reaction to Communist dictatorship. Across the decade and a half after the transition to democracy in Central and Eastern Europe, trust in three of the four principal political institutions—the courts, the political parties, the executive, and the parliament—dropped by an average of almost 10 percent, but only political parties elicited lower levels of trust overall than parliaments. The executive is the most trusted institution, followed by the courts, in part because they appear to act decisively as, in comparison to legislatures, their decision-making processes are largely hidden from public view.[22]

Public attitudes toward legislatures reflect what is most visible about them, which means they are driven by legislatures' policy decisions or indecisions on those issues to which the public pays attention and on which it has clear views. But few issues attract wide public attention, and most are so complicated that public understanding of them is partial at best. Undoubtedly, a general public frustration with policy problems drives attitudes toward legislatures; partisanship may also be a factor, and the cabinet-formation process may be frustratingly time-consuming. Yet, there is evidence of a very generalized support for the maintenance of a legislature in the abstract, apart from a particular membership and the issues of the moment. This is true even where the legislature is a new institution. In developing countries, the institution attracts traditional forms of respect for legislators as patrons. In newly democratic countries, legislatures symbolize the end of authoritarian rule. Where they have long existed, their continued existence is unquestioned.

Even though legislatures' relatively low popularity therefore does not threaten their survival anywhere, it does have implications for their role in governance. In the United States it prompts public efforts to limit legislative salaries, staffs, and terms. It feeds distrust of the professionalization of legislatures, sustains a nostalgia for the citizen legislator, and thereby undercuts the capacity of legislatures to hold their own with interest groups and executives. In Europe, the low popularity of legislatures has eroded a once relatively high level of participation in parliamentary elections. Yet, despite all of this evidence of public distrust of the institution and frustration over its behavior, these negative attitudes do not seem to undermine acceptance of the institution in most countries as it did in Europe in the 1920s and 1930s.

Combating Public Distrust with Greater Transparency

Although the survival of legislatures in the age of their worldwide proliferation is not in doubt, evidence of the public's negative attitude toward them is compelling and troubling. Recent research suggests that even more visible about legislatures than their policy decisions or indecisions is the process by which they make them, not the substance of the decisions themselves. This process displays controversy and compromise, slow, ponderous, and arcane decision making, the influence of special interests, and apparently insincere posturing among antagonists. Most visible about legislatures is also that they constitute very large collections of individuals distinguished from their constituents by being professional politicians, usually setting their own salaries and benefits, and spending most of their time in venues other than the televised sessions that interested members of the public can watch. None of this is attractive to the casual citizen observer, convinced that there is a solution to every political controversy if only politicians would find it. Worse, compared to executive, judicial, military, and private institutions, controversy in the legislature is very visible. The available evidence of the low popularity of legislatures may therefore be rooted in some basic characteristics of the institution, in the way in which legislatures work very openly but also just beneath the surface in committee meetings, caucuses, and informal contacts. Much of what legislatures do very publicly seems staged, and that which they do just beneath the surface provides grounds for public suspicion, incomprehension, cynicism, and distrust.

The implication of the electoral connection is that voters must be able to hold their representatives accountable. That means that they must be able to see what legislators and legislatures do. Consequently, there is pressure for meetings of the legislature and its committees to be open, subject to public scrutiny. Democratic representativeness implies transparency. The German parliament, especially sensitive to the need for public support in view of the troubled history of parliamentary government in that country, went so far as to embody the principle of transparency in the architecture of the Reichstag building when it was renovated in 1999. The parliamentary chamber is enclosed by transparent walls, opening it to light and to public view. The pinnacle of the building is a transparent dome, open to visitors, from which they can look down and see the chamber in session (see Figure 4.1).

The U.S. House of Representatives permitted television coverage of its proceedings beginning in 1979, and the cable networks established C-Span to provide that coverage. Other legislatures were at first reluctant to open their proceedings to the camera, but toward the end of the twentieth century, many of them, including both the most established and the newest national legislatures, accepted coverage. Televised sessions now exist in over thirty national legislatures. But the result is often the display of empty chambers, addressed by a small group of members, since so much of legislative business takes place in committees or party caucuses. And that leaves the average citizen baffled and distressed. After the sessions of the British House of Commons were opened to television, four out of five respondents to a survey said that their view of Parliament had declined as a result of watching the debates.[23] Getting transparency right is a Goldilocks problem: not too little but also not too much.

Tension exists between this need for openness and the realization that openness feeds public dismay. Transparency displays to the public all of the characteristics of legislative proceedings that run counter to its expectations: time-consuming bargaining

Figure 4.1 The Reichstag (© Deutscher Bundestag / MELDEPRESS / Sylvia Bohn)

among large numbers of decision makers, compromise among
points of view that often entails compromise of principles, insincere courtesy among members trying to mute personal conflict,
and complex, counterintuitive procedures. This very transparency is the source of public distrust.

Legislators have always been inclined to obscure some parts
of their decision-making processes by closing some committee
meetings and most political-party meetings. The early parliaments did not publish their proceedings at all because, although
members always regarded themselves as representatives of their
constituencies, they were nervous about having their views, let

alone their votes, made public. In Great Britain votes were not reported until the end of the seventeenth century, and debates were not published until early in the nineteenth.[24] In the U.S. House of Representatives, votes in the Committee of the Whole, where many of the important decisions were taken, were not recorded until 1971. The use of recorded votes varies greatly among legislatures and over time, but it has become more prevalent. But in today's age of ever greater openness, members of legislatures still find ways to hide the bargaining that takes place between the executive and the legislature and between interest groups and legislators. That is why so little of importance happens on the floor of the legislature, where the public view is focused.

Achieving the right balance between openness and confidentiality in deliberation is the subject of John R. Hibbing and Elizabeth Theiss-Morse's *Congress As Public Enemy*. They write that "Congress is . . . viewed by the public as an enemy . . . *because* it is so public."[25] They suggest that the public has stronger preferences about the appropriate political process than about particular policy outcomes. The public's preference proceeds from the assumption that a common interest can be discovered on most political issues, and political conflict is unnecessary if political decisions are made by "empathetic, non-self-interested decision makers." Most Americans, Hibbing and Theiss-Morse write, would prefer a political process that requires only occasional popular participation in decisions.[26] Recent research in Germany yields similar conclusions. Helmar Schöne finds that it is the process that is distrusted. From research with focus groups of candidates for teaching positions and college students, he provides evidence that attitudes toward parliament reflect "prejudice against conflict and quarreling [and] dissatisfaction with lengthy, inscrutable decision-making processes in which the interests of various groups on the one hand, and the interests of the elected politicians on the other, must be taken into account."[27] The unwillingness of citizens to recognize that political issues are bound to be controversial leads to criticism of the

institutions that display those controversies. In democratic societies those are typically the political parties and the legislature,
which exhibit their controversies most visibly.

Public frustration with legislatures has manifested itself from
time to time in a rejection of the principle of representation
itself, first expressed fundamentally by Jean-Jacques Rousseau in
his classic work *On the Social Contract*:

> Sovereignty cannot be represented. . . . It consists essentially of the
> general will and will cannot be represented. Either it is itself or it
> is different. There is no middle term. The Deputies of the People
> are not, nor can they be, its representatives. They can only be its
> commissioners. . . . Laws which the people have not ratified in
> their own person are null and void.[28]

The institutional manifestation of that view regards legislatures
as basically illegitimate. It is related to a variety of forms of direct
democracy, notably the popular initiative and the referendum.
Direct democracy has a long and venerable history in the small
communes of Switzerland, which Rousseau admired, and in
New England town meetings, which have had no similarly illus-
trious exponent. But direct democracy has had a checkered
history in Europe, where the Napoleonic use of the plebiscite
and the referendum first demonstrated its authoritarian possibilities. In twentieth-century Europe, dictatorships used referenda
and plebiscites to demonstrate their legitimacy. But democracies
have also used them from time to time to resolve issues that cut
across the lines of the party system, most recently in various
stages of the construction of the European Union.[29]

At the state level in the United States, the initiative and the
referendum were the favored instruments of early twentieth-century reformers anxious to bypass legislatures that they regarded as
controlled by political bosses. In the twenty-first century, provisions for popular referenda on legislation exist in twenty-four of
the U.S. states, and provisions for popular legislative initiatives
exist in nineteen of them. The policy consequences of these
instruments of direct democracy give citizens' groups the ability

to enact legislation that reflects the interest of a momentary majority but does not take minority interests into account and often has unintended long-term consequences. They also give conservative economic groups means to solidify the influence that they have within the legislature by enacting constitutional restrictions on legislative majorities. The superior ability of both kinds of interest groups to formulate issues and to turn out the votes of their adherents gives them special political influence, contrary to the intention of the progressive reformers who created these instruments.[30] In California, where the initiative and the referendum have often immobilized the legislature, a majority of the public regularly expresses confidence that policy decisions made by the initiative process are better than decisions made by the legislature.[31] Thus, from Rousseau's principled argument in the eighteenth century to the intermittent uses of plebiscites, popular initiatives, and referenda ever since, the penchant for direct democracy, side by side with the ubiquitous existence of legislatures, manifests the recurring public distrust of the legislative institution.

Public Support for New Legislatures

Should we be concerned by the contrast between the apparent indispensability of legislatures in all political systems and public distrust of those aspects of the political process that are distinctive to them? If this is a cause for concern, can anything be done about it? Public support for legislatures is especially critical where they are relatively new, where they are not taken for granted, and where in the past they have occasionally been abolished. But even where their historical roots are not deep, public acceptance, if not active support, is surprisingly strong. Research on public attitudes toward legislatures in twelve post-Communist states in Central and Eastern Europe shows that in the first decade and a half of their election in multiparty contests, public acceptance of the somewhat unfamiliar institution was high.

Attachment was strongest in the countries of Central Europe and somewhat weaker in the countries that had been part of the Soviet Union. But confidence in the survival of elected parliaments grew the longer they existed. The proportion of the population hoping that parliaments would be abolished declined steadily.[32]

The experience of Central and Eastern Europe is not duplicated in postcolonial Africa, even though there, too, there are very few instances of the abolition of parliaments once they have been established. In Africa legislatures bear the mark of the colonial experience, dominated by the president in a continuation of patrimonial rule and in the absence of strong political parties. The ability of legislatures to develop an independent political role under these circumstances has depended on the determination of a small group of reformers within the legislature, including its officers, acting with the support of civil society organizations outside the legislature. Such a "coalition for change" has in a few countries provided incentives for members of parliament to bring about amendments in the electoral system, the rules of procedure, legislative salaries, and legislative staffing. That has strengthened the role of the legislatures in these countries, even in the absence of widespread public support. But the most comprehensive study of the development of legislatures in Africa concludes that it has so far been a slow, internally driven process relying on a small group of reformers who have achieved only "fragile gains." On the basis of case studies of six African legislatures, Joel Barkan writes that "the common finding . . . is that legislative performance is highly uneven."[33]

Can Public Understanding of Legislatures Be Improved?

If the survival of parliaments is not of immediate concern, the misunderstanding of legislatures, the propensity of the mass public to criticize or ignore them, diminishes their significance in the political system everywhere. There is a troubling gap between the way legislatures are understood in specialized publics—in political science, in journals of political analysis, and by specialized publics organized as interest groups—and the way they are portrayed in the popular media and in surveys of national opinion. Newspaper and television accounts of legislatures tend to publicize scandals in which individual members are involved and to stress policy conflicts among representatives. To the extent that they express strong policy positions, newspapers and television commentators disparage the sharply opposing views of the members and regard compromise cynically. Time and space are usually too limited to give adequate coverage to complicated policy issues. The public misunderstanding of legislatures feeds public distrust of politics and politicians, which has been growing in all countries over the last generation. Standard projects of civic education, of explaining constitutional provisions, encouraging voting participation, and discussing issues in town meetings and classrooms, probably make some contribution to an understanding of legislatures. But in view of the evidence that the public prefers what Hibbing and Theiss-Morse call "stealth democracy," by which they mean a political system that does not require too much public attention most of the time, these scholars are skeptical of the standard projects of civic education. They write,

> The most promising, but not easily implemented proposal, is to educate citizens better on the need to tolerate conflict in a highly diverse, complex, modern democratic political system. Only then will people better appreciate the usefulness of institutional arrangements that try to put together solutions by listening to many voices, including those of special interests, debating all sides of the issue, and compromising to reach a solution agreeable to many.[34]

There are analogies between collective decision making in legislatures and in settings familiar to citizens outside politics. Most people can reflect on their experience with collective decisions in nongovernmental settings, in civil society. It is in these settings that most people experience the social dilemmas that arise whenever they try to move from individual preferences to collective decisions. These are the same dilemmas that lie at the heart of the work of legislatures. Civic education could use familiar examples of the problem of collective decision making, encouraging participants to reflect on the need to devise agendas that narrow choices, to devise procedures for decisions, to recognize the advantages of specialization, and to apply these reflections to examples drawn from decisions in families, interest associations, friendships groups, churches, professions, schools, and offices. This would be a way of drawing on what Robert Putnam has called the "social capital"[35] that exists in most cultures in order to understand by analogy what decision making in legislative politics entails.

Across all the variation that exists in the roles that contemporary legislatures play in systems of government, the common thread is that they provide linkage between the public and the government. Even the most authoritarian governments rely on legislatures to provide links to the public, despite permitting little public influence on government. The effectiveness of legislatures, no matter how small or how large, depends on some public understanding of the institution. The most fundamental puzzle posed by this institution is how to make it understandable by the public it is supposed to represent. There is a sharp contrast between the appreciation of legislatures in the community of legislative scholars and the disparagement of the institution in the mass media and public opinion. That contrast could be diminished if some aspects of the professional literature were accessible to a wider audience. In the next chapter, I turn to a survey of the professional literature that reflects the methods of legislative research developed in the last half century.

CHAPTER FIVE
WAYS OF STUDYING LEGISLATURES

S cholars undertake research in any field because they are puzzled by a phenomenon that interests them. The long history
of legislatures has attracted successive generations of historians,
philosophers, lawyers, and political scientists, who wish to
understand this venerable institution and are puzzled by its
endurance, the variety of its manifestations, its adaptability to
different times and political contexts, and its apparent contradictions, which I have noted in the preceding chapters.

In the long history of the study of legislatures, the last half
century has been particularly productive. In political science,
legislative research has not suffered the methodological controversies that have afflicted other subfields of the discipline. To be
sure, the generally favored research approaches have changed
from time to time, reflecting changes in other subfields of the
discipline. But at any given moment, a variety of methods has
been accepted, and there has never been wholesale rejection of
any method of study. The reason for this benign state of affairs
is that there is general agreement on what the subject of legislative research should be. Legislatures are well-defined institutions
with some common characteristics in all their historical and
geographic settings. Their functions and relationships to other
institutions vary over time and space, but there is no dispute

about their defining characteristics: they are collections of members who are nominally equal to each other, they presume to represent others, and they exert influence on government by various means such as lawmaking, executive oversight, the recruitment of political executives, and the legitimating of governmental decisions.

Legislatures are preeminently rule-governed institutions. That they consist of a large number of members of formally equal status makes rules indispensable to their organization. The study of legislatures has always examined what they do, their functions in the political system, their inputs and outputs, the origin of the items on their agendas, and their accomplishments. It has involved investigation of their members, their recruitment, their demographic characteristics, and their careers. It has a historical dimension, reaching back to study the evolution of the institution. But because legislatures are so significantly rule governed, their study has always focused on the rules that organize their activities, formal and informal. These rules derive from custom or from constitutional or legal enactments and consist of norms governing behavior and rules of the game. They also hold the key to explaining the puzzle of what makes it possible for a large collection of nominally equal members to reach decisions.

The Focus on U.S. Legislatures

As the discipline of political science developed in the United States, legislative studies became a subfield of the study of American politics, focused primarily on the U.S. Congress and, somewhat subordinately, on state and local legislatures in the United States. Among legislative scholars in the United States, a research community developed in the 1950s and 1960s consisting of a cohort of young scholars mentored at a few universities. This community was continually reinforced by conferences and informal meetings and by the establishment of a legislative-studies section in the American Political Science Association (APSA), informally in 1977 and as a formal organization six years later. One of the larger sections within the APSA, consisting of over six hundred members, the section has organized the panels on legislative research for the annual meetings of the APSA, awards prizes for the best dissertations, papers, articles, and books in the field, and provides to its members a subscription to the *Legislative Studies Quarterly*, its official scholarly journal.

In the field of comparative politics, which focused primarily on European political systems until the middle of the twentieth century, there was work on the parliaments of individual countries, usually on their role in the parliamentary system of government. After World War II, the field of comparative politics extended its purview to the developing areas of the world, and legislative research expanded to include developing legislatures, research encouraged by grants from the Ford Foundation and the U.S. Agency for International Development.[1] Studies of particular legislatures had normative concerns, led by questions about how important the legislature was in the political system and what functions it performed. Research that compared legislatures using a theoretical framework abstracted from their settings in a particular country or time was rare.[2] Thus, research on legislatures throughout most of the twentieth century consisted primarily of research on particular legislatures, first and foremost the U.S. Congress, and even more narrowly on the House of Representatives. Secondarily, there was research on U.S. state legislatures. The heavy emphasis on American legislatures began to change in the last third of the twentieth century as a result of efforts by a small group of scholars to promote comparative legislative research in developing countries, facilitated by grant-supported research conferences, with a focus on the role of legislatures in democratization. Comparative research on legislatures in the older democracies broadened in the last decade of the twentieth century with the development of abstract models of legislative processes, a subject to which I return below.

The baseline for research on Congress in the middle of the twentieth century was a large volume of work on its constitutional powers, rules of procedure, and legislative enactments, as well as proposals for its reform. There had been regular reports on the work of each session of the U.S. Congress in *The American Political Science Review*. There had been Woodrow Wilson's interpretation of Congress as a committee-dominated, decentralized institution. There was Stuart Rice's innovative work on roll call votes.[3] There were studies of the influence of interest groups in Congress. But the weight of congressional research had been on legal powers and procedures and on legislative enactments, work often aided and abetted by members of the staff of Congress. So, Congress had certainly received substantial attention from political science from the beginning of its professional organization. But a survey of the field by Nelson Polsby and Eric Schickler, two of its foremost practitioners, found "a sharp upturn after World War II in the number and quality of books and articles that focused on the political behavior of Congress rather than its legal and constitutional powers, its administrative machinery, or its alleged inadequacies as a vessel of responsible party government."[4]

Three influences produced this outpouring of work on Congress. The first was the Congressional Fellowship Program, founded by the American Political Science Association in 1953, which gave young political scientists the opportunity to spend ten months on the staff of a member of Congress or a congressional committee and to observe Congress from the inside, a rare research opportunity, especially at a time when the work of Congress was not as open as it became after the reforms of the 1970s. Over a half century, about seven hundred young scholars have participated in this program, which influenced many of their long-term research agendas. Its alumni include such eventually influential scholars as David Mayhew, Thomas Mann, David W. Rohde, Bruce Oppenheimer, Lawrence Dodd, Barbara Sinclair, and Steven S. Smith.[5] The program expanded from its beginning to include also a large number of journalists, policy specialists, civil servants, and foreign political writers.

The second influence, ten years after the start of the Congressional Fellowship Program, was a grant, solicited by the American Political Science Association from the Carnegie Corporation, for a "Study of Congress," a project initially involving several members of Congress but then entirely organized by scholars. It eventually produced a series of books designed to fill the "large gaps in what political scientists know about Congress."[6] These were empirical studies of the legislative process, the seniority system, and the committee and party organization of Congress, but though they reflected a sociological style that distinguished them from previous work on Congress, they did not reflect any methodological orthodoxy. Many of them did reflect, however, a penchant for quantification and regression analysis and tests of statistical significance. The series of books and articles that resulted from the "Study of Congress" project produced a fairly comprehensive description of the institution, which was subsequently called "the textbook Congress." The descriptions are dated in two respects: Their authors had observed Congress before the major reforms of the institution in the 1970s, when its work was decentralized and committee centered, and the authors approached their subject without any overriding theory.[7]

The third influence producing the large volume of work on Congress in the post–World War II period was methodological. It was the "behavioral persuasion" that had taken hold in many parts of the discipline, a reaction against the "legal-institutional" emphasis in political science. Scholars of this persuasion urged that the unit of observation in the study of politics should be the individual actor—the voter, the legislator, the party member, the leader. "The political behavior of the individual person is the central and crucial empirical datum of the behavioral approaches to politics," wrote Heinz Eulau, one of the methodology's intellectual leaders.[8] This focus on the individual actor was applied principally to citizens' voting behavior, leading to the publication of the enormously influential study titled *The American Voter*.[9] The focus on the behavior of the individual also affected research on legislators. The excitement generated by this new emphasis, coupled with access to the recommended "unit of observation"—the member of the legislature, the constituent, the leader—greatly stimulated one type of legislative research. Data on the individual member became increasingly available as a result of the work of the Congressional Research Service, the record-keeping provided by the *Congressional Quarterly*'s publications, and computerized records of members' roll call votes. In short, legislative research flowered in the third quarter of the twentieth century, spurred in part by the professional organization of the discipline and in part by intellectual developments in the profession. But legislative research remained largely directed to the study of the U.S. Congress.

The Micropolitical Approach

The micropolitical approach recommended by the behavioral persuasion in political science sought to explain the legislative institution from individual-level data, gathered from social-background information on members, survey data on constituents' beliefs, participant observation, and interviews with legislators. Motivating this approach was the puzzle of how a group of individuals interacted to systematically produce a collective result. The support of the Social Science Research Council in response to four entirely separate grant applications from four young legislative scholars, most of whom did not know each other, resulted in *The Legislative System*, the highly influential interview study of the legislatures of California, New Jersey, Ohio, and Tennessee, to which I referred in chapter 2 with reference to its relevance to research on representation. Encouraged by the Council to coordinate their research, the four—John C. Wahlke, Heinz Eulau, William Buchanan, and Leroy C. Ferguson—met repeatedly to design a single project. They conducted their interviews with 474 members of these legislatures separately, each in their home state, using an agreed-upon interview schedule to construct the legislators' role orientations. The authors found in the sociological concept of role a "model of the individual legislator [which] relates the behavior of legislators to problems of legislative structure and function, which are the traditional concern of students of the field." The lead author wrote, "The concept of a role associated with a position of membership in any institutionalized group refers to precisely those behavioral uniformities or regularities which constitute the institution."[10]

The authors distinguished legislators' purposive roles, representational roles, areal roles, pressure group roles, and party roles, constructing from these role orientations what they called the legislative system.[11] They set out their interview schedules, procedures, coding categories, and methods for constructing their concepts from the interview data in great detail in six appendices occupying thirty-nine pages, contributing to the replication of their research by others.[12]

The authors of *The Legislative System* were aware that the analysis of individual-level data on legislative studies was quite different from that of survey data on large populations. How, for example, could they deal with problems of significance? They had interviewed nearly all of the members of four state legislatures of various sizes. Could they generalize from their observations beyond the four legislatures they had studied to some universe of legislatures? If so, how could they demonstrate the significance of their inferences from the legislators they had observed to the universe of legislators? If not, could they at least generalize across the four bicameral legislatures whose members they had observed by weighting the responses of members to take account of the different sizes of the eight houses to which these members belonged? If they could not presume to engage in the kinds of generalizations that students of voting behavior undertook by making inferences from random samples to large populations, were they limited to conclusions that applied only to four state legislatures at one moment in time?[13]

Within less than a decade of the publication of the four-state study, the limits of this approach for explaining legislative behavior became clear in the United States, quite apart from the limits of the generalizability of its findings in the statistical sense. Malcolm E. Jewell surveyed role analysis as early as the end of the decade of the 1960s and found "the evidence concerning possible sources of legislative roles fragmentary and sometimes contradictory." He noted that "the value of role analysis for most political scientists lies in its potential for improving explanation and prediction of legislative behavior," but he went on to write that "as yet, this is a potential that remains largely unrealized in practice."[14] Nevertheless, he saw potential for role analysis in cross-national research because the description of roles and the evidence of a consensus on role orientations among members of a legislature might be a measure of its institutionalization and its functions in the political system.[15] Indeed, role analysis continued in legislative research outside the United States long after it was essentially abandoned in the study of American legislatures. Since it was readily possible to reproduce the American study by adapting its interview schedule to different legislatures, replications were numerous.[16] A large literature on the role conceptions of German legislators developed under the leadership of Werner Patzelt and has been carried on by many of his students. "The concept of role is applicable to entirely differently structured parliaments," Jürgen von Oertzen, one of Patzelt's students, wrote as he called for more intensive studies of role concepts in other parliaments.[17] There have been role-theoretical studies of legislatures in Canada, France, Hungary, and Singapore, in an Indian state, and in the European Parliament.[18]

Role theory served as the framework for a major study of the British House of Commons by Donald D. Searing, published in 1994, begun in the heyday of role analysis in the early 1970s, but not completed until a quarter century later.[19] Searing prefaced it with a chapter in which he sought to rescue role analysis by a review of the various uses to which it had been put and the various conceptual confusions that had hurt it. But Searing recognized that "role theory is not a theory"[20] but a descriptive framework. It was never clear just how a set of roles combines into a legislative system or can be said to comprise the legislative institution. Although role analysis continues to be used to describe newly democratic legislatures in Central and Eastern Europe, Africa, and Asia, it is no longer the mainstream of legislative research.

The micropolitical approach, epitomized for a time by role analysis, had another existence in the "participant-observation" method exemplified by Richard F. Fenno Jr.'s *Home Style*. What at first sight appeared to be an extremely thorough description of the activity of eighteen members of the U.S. House of Representatives in their constituencies—but merely a description—was really a creative conceptualization of how legislators see their constituencies and how their perception affects their legislative work. This connection between members' "home style" and "Hill style" became a template for using "thick description" of the individual legislators as data for explaining collective outcomes in the legislature. In part because Fenno's approach had deceptively modest methodological objectives and in part because he carried it out with such a profound understanding of the culture of the legislative institution, his work became a classic in the discipline, often cited but rarely imitated. One could infer from it that observation at the micropolitical level could yield macropolitical explanations. But participant observation requires extraordinary skills and time— Fenno's research for *Home Style* occupied him for over seven years. Furthermore, as Fenno himself realized, it raised a series of methodological issues.[21] Helmar Schöne noted one of them, as a result of his use of participant observation in German legislatures. He realized that legislators often cannot articulate many aspects of their work—for example, informal rules—because usually an actor cannot articulate that which he takes for granted.[22] But once he or she recognizes this, the participant observer can gain a better understanding of this aspect of a legislator's behavior than an interview study could yield.

The Turn to a Macropolitical Approach

"Fenno's paradox," his observation that we love our Congressman so much more than our Congress, is a reminder that attitudes toward Congress are not just the sum of attitudes toward each of its members, because Congress is not just the sum of its parts. Participant observation did not explicitly address what Heinz Eulau called the "micro-macro dilemmas in political science."[23] Ever since his work on the role analysis of members of four state legislatures, Eulau was conscious of the fact that "as political scientists we are not just interested in similarities or differences in individual behavior, but in their consequences 'for the functioning of larger groups and institutions.'" He went on to say that "analysis carried out exclusively at the level of individuals . . . cannot come to grips with the consequences of political structures for political action."[24] Eulau continued to grapple with this subject, rightly subtitling his collection of essays on it "Personal Pathways Through Complexity." In his clearest discussion of the methodological problems of measuring and analyzing aggregate properties and relating that analysis to observations at the individual level, Eulau offered a diagram that distinguished between levels of analysis and levels of observation.[25] He reflected on the need to transform data gathered at one level to make them applicable to analysis at another level. Eulau's contribution was to make scholars aware of the need to distinguish among levels of observation and analysis when analyzing the legislative institution and its representational properties. His work made the field of legislative research newly sensitive to the danger of making inferences about collective properties from micropolitical data. He had been one of the forerunners of the "behavioral persuasion," which directed so much attention to observation of individuals. But he never lost sight of the fact that the legislative institution had collective properties that needed to be studied in their own right. This was recognized most fully by rational-choice theory and formal modeling, an approach that has come to dominate legislative research in the United States.

The impetus came from two directions, first of all from developments in the subject itself. The major reform of Congress in the 1970s, beginning with the Legislative Reorganization Act of 1970, turned scholars' attention once again to the rules of the institution, because changes undertaken in the rules, both formal and informal, significantly altered the distribution of influence within the institution and called attention to members' goals and purposes.[26] Second, it came from two methodological directions, both of which produced a renewal of the discipline's traditional interest in the study of institutions. One direction came from scholars in the long-established field of organization theory, who emphasized the consequences of how political life is organized for the actions of individuals.[27] But the interest in political institutions came most importantly from a new direction taken by a small group of scholars impressed by the way formal modeling had been employed in economics to study strategic interactions. The method of developing an abstract, stylized version of an object of study in order to focus, laser-like, on a few of its aspects seemed eminently applicable to the study of complex political institutions. For political scientists interested in legislatures, it produced a focus on the rules that constrain the behavior of legislators and an assumption of "rationality [as] the principal modeling flavor of choice," as Kenneth Shepsle put it. Modeling legislative processes seemed ideally suited to the study of a rule-governed institution composed of calculating, purposeful actors interacting with each other.[28]

The attraction of "rational-choice institutionalism" for legislative research was threefold. First, it called attention to the formal and informal rules that constitute the legislative institution. Second, it provided a way of examining how self-interested legislators serving their individual policy and reelection objectives could accept the constraints imposed by rules and customs to achieve collective results. And third, it offered a way of explaining the stability of the legislative institution by postulating that at any given moment the rules governing the behavior of the members stand in equilibrium with each other, that they hang together until a major external event disrupts them.

Just as previous methods of studying legislatures were spurred by contingent events—the APSA's establishment of the Congressional Fellowship Program, the Carnegie Corporation's "Study of Congress" grant, the Social Science Research Council's grant for a study of four state legislatures—so the advent of rational-choice institutionalism in legislative studies was shaped by a contingent event, the development of William Riker's research and teaching at the University of Rochester. What Riker called "positive political theory," by which he meant non-normative theory, "looks to individual decision making as the source of collective political outcomes and postulates that the individual functions according to the logic of rational self-interest."[29] Riker's goal, and the goal of the influential students he trained, notably Kenneth Shepsle and Barry R. Weingast, was to formulate abstract models of political behavior, formally expressed in mathematical terms, that could be explored to solve the puzzle of how the self-interested actions of individuals could produce stable political outcomes.[30] Riker was influenced by a number of propositions derived from the mathematical theory of games, among them that majority rule with sincere voting leads to the cycling of preferences among multidimensional choices. Riker faced the challenge of explaining how the constraints imposed by rules and structures avoid the chaos that would exist in legislatures without them, and how an equilibrium is achieved among possible choices. This led him to explore the limits that political institutions impose on choices, notably by the setting of an agenda, by channeling decisions by means of voting rules and committee privileges, and by strategic voting. His approach was ideally suited to research on legislatures because they could readily be conceptualized as institutions composed of self-interested, purposeful members taking strategic actions within a set of rules to achieve their purposes. A succession of Riker's students derived new, empirically testable insights into the organization and procedures of legislatures by viewing legislative behavior in this sense as a game following explicit rules.

Rational-choice institutionalism gave renewed attention to legislative rules and organization, now seen not in their traditional historical or legalistic terms but as structures making possible stable, collective outcomes from legislators' individual preferences. While the impetus came from a single scholar, it was solidified by the political science department he developed at the University of Rochester, by his students whose influence spread throughout the political science profession in the United States, by the Public Choice Society and its journal, *Public Choice*, and by a cross-disciplinary professional group of economists, mathematicians, sociologists, philosophers, and specialists in public administration and public finance.

New Impetus for Cross-National and Diachronic Research

While this method of studying legislatures has become the dominant mode in the United States, it has had to overcome three limitations: It was originally applied almost exclusively to studies of the U.S. House of Representatives, it originally ignored structural change over time or across institutions, and it developed a jargon that made it inaccessible to much of the broader research community. For a generation it attracted principally students of the U.S. Congress, or even more narrowly, of the U.S. House of Representatives, and its transferability to other legislatures was not explored. In that way it suffered from the general parochialism of legislative research in the United States. What Gerald Gamm and John Huber called "the standard template for Congressional research on institutions" tended to dominate modeling even of legislatures outside the United States.[31] But that has been changing. There has been a growing tendency among scholars both in the United States and elsewhere to apply rational-choice methods to cross-national legislative studies. Three examples from a large new body of research suggest the possibilities. Gary W. Cox analyzed the stability of the rules of legislatures across systems, comparing those that are entrenched in a constitution, as in France, to those that can only be changed by qualified majorities, as in many European and Latin American countries, to those that are changeable by majorities in the very legislatures they are supposed to constrain. He found that legislative leaders are reluctant to change rules under most circumstances, regardless of how they are entrenched, because it takes time and effort to change them, and because they provide leaders with control over the agenda, the voting procedure, and the outcomes, without being very obvious or challengeable by constituents.[32] Huber compared restrictive rules for setting the agenda in the U.S. House of Representatives and the French National Assembly and explained how, in different ways, each enables the majority party (or "the government") to control the agenda.[33] As these two examples imply, cross-national research can show that institutional needs of legislatures, such as agenda control, may be achieved by different means in different settings, but variation in settings is more likely to affect the form of rules than their effects. Other cross-national research enumerates nation-specific differences in legislative procedures. Bjørn Erik Rasch analyzed the difference between the amendment procedure used in most Anglo-Saxon countries and the successive voting procedure used in most of Europe. He showed that these procedures have different consequences and appear to result from different histories.[34]

The attraction of American research universities to young scholars in other countries has brought legislative specialists from Europe, Latin America, and Asia into contact with the research methods that became prevalent in political science in the United States. This has led them to apply formal models to the study of legislatures within their own nations and across countries. In the last decade, therefore, the rational-choice framework has been applied to comparative legislative research both by American scholars and by scholars in other countries, and this has helped to overcome the parochialism that characterized the approach originally.

Models, while they are stylized abstractions of legislative structures and processes, are not necessarily context free. For example, Keith Krehbiel's model of pivotal politics assumes that the preferences of legislators can be arrayed along a unidimensional policy space and that political parties play no role in organizing legislators' preferences.[35] These are not assumptions that Europeanists or Latin Americanists would make. Adapting Krehbiel's approach to Latin American legislatures is not impossible, but it would have to take account of differences not only in constitutional systems but in the dimensionality of issues, electoral systems, and the incentives of politicians.[36] This requires close acquaintance with differences in political contexts and confronts the problem that American scholars are often less acquainted with legislative research outside the United States than non-Americans are with legislative studies in the United States. Therefore, collaboration between American and non-American scholars has proven particularly valuable. Recent work on Latin American legislatures has done just that. And when scholars pay attention to cultural contexts, they can achieve what comparative politics can ideally accomplish: the determination of what aspects of the differences among legislatures are due to irreducible differences in their national settings.

Another attraction of cross-national research is that it can contribute to designing empirical tests for what are often highly abstract models. Different models often lead to observationally equivalent predictions. For example, the debate over whether legislative committees or the majority party or parties control legislatures' agendas generated controversy for a decade because it was difficult to design a test using roll call data that would disconfirm either proposition. A substantial literature exhibits that controversy.[37] To the extent that models developed in the American setting are then applied to legislatures in other countries, they have been subject to robust tests. John Huber's work on the French National Assembly and the research of Kenneth Shepsle and Michael Laver on the making and breaking of coalitions provide two examples.[38] Some hypotheses have been tested with data across many national settings—for example, Carol Mershon's research on the variable transaction costs entailed in remaking coalitions and Douglas Dion's tests of his counterintuitive hypothesis that small rather than large legislative majorities are inclined to restrict minority rights.[39] The most intriguing formal models of legislative processes are those that yield counterintuitive hypotheses that can be tested with cross-national data.

Having increasingly departed from the "the standard template for Congressional research on institutions,"[40] which was the initial limitation of the rational-choice approach, it faces a second limitation in its often implicit assumption that the institutional setting, the rules that structure behavior, is fixed. This assumption also reflects the origin of the rational-choice approach in congressional studies, which usually, though not always, neglected the historical dimension, the effect of change over time. For legislatures outside the United States, however, some of the most interesting questions concern the effect of institutional change. There is, of course, no reason why change over time cannot be modeled. By now a substantial formal modeling literature exists on the development of legislatures to address the puzzle of "why particular institutions exist, evolve and survive."[41] For example, theories based on formal models have been used to explain the important aspects of the evolution of the British parliament, such as the delegation of appropriations power from Parliament to the Government in the seventeenth century and the appearance of cabinet dominance in the nineteenth century.[42]

A third limitation of the rational-choice approach is similar to the obstacle that language has always posed to cross-national legislative research. From the start and increasingly, the commitment to abstract mathematical models has led its practitioners to speak and write in the language of mathematics and logical symbols, creating problems of translation for scholars unfamiliar with that language. At the same time, since it is not nation specific, this is actually an advantage in cross-national communication, even while it is a barrier to scholarly communication across methods of inquiry. But language differences also reflect differences in research cultures. Direct translation from the language of mathematics to ordinary language or from formal notation to the familiar alphabet may be as difficult as translation across ordinary languages. Clearly students seriously interested in doing formal modeling must learn its language. But it is important to preserve the sense of community among legislative scholars across all methodological persuasions that has served this subfield so well. This depends on having explanations of the work in formal modeling expressed also in ordinary language.

When eminent legislative specialists Kenneth Shepsle and David Rohde discussed the role of American political science in the field of legislative studies a decade ago, Shepsle recalls that they agreed that "despite the exceptionalism of its history and institutional practices, American politics has served the wider political science community by forging scientific tools and providing a laboratory in which they are tested, perfected, and prepared for export."[43] From this perspective, legislative research as it developed in the United States in the last half century can escape the charge of parochialism and the criticism that it has stood in the way of a genuinely comparative study of legislatures. Its long-run contribution has been to methods of inquiry that are not necessarily culture bound.

By its focus on the rules of the game, formal modeling has been responsible for a renewal of a macropolitical approach to legislative studies. Because the approach attracts the theoretically inclined scholar, formal modelers are often as uninterested in applying models to empirical verification just as empiricists are indifferent to the theoretical implications of their findings. In that respect the advent of formal modeling does not overcome the familiar division between theory and observation that has always existed in the discipline. In part this is a function of scholarly tastes, of the relative preference for developing abstract theories as opposed to observation and statistical analysis. Some journals in the field have required authors of articles that employ formal models to include empirical tests of their models to nudge theorists and empiricists closer together.

The development of methods of legislative research can be seen as an evolution from methods of macropolitical analysis, of studying the institution as a whole in terms of its legal and constitutional framework, to microanalytical analysis of its members, their perceptions, their role concepts, and their actions, and then once again to the study of the institution as a whole, modeled as a set of rules in which actors pursue strategies in a game in which each intends to prevail. But this evolution is not merely a cyclical alteration governed by intellectual fashions. It is rather a development that has used methodological innovations to bring new foci to an unchanging commitment to understanding the legislative institution, to solving the puzzles it presents. It has not been marked by sharp controversies among practitioners of different methods but rather by normal intellectual controversies within a community of scholars in which common scholarly interests, buttressed by common professional organizations, are a source of cohesion. The micropolitical approach exemplified by role-theoretical analysis and participant observation has sought to explain the aggregate properties of legislatures with evidence from individual-level behavior, while the rational-choice approach has used evidence from the rules and structures that constitute legislatures' aggregate properties to explain individual-level behavior. In this sense the two approaches that have dominated legislative research in the last generation are complementary.

CHAPTER SIX
HAS SCHOLARSHIP UNRAVELED
THE PUZZLES OF LEGISLATURES?

Although historians, lawyers, sociologists, and students of politics have long been fascinated by legislatures, the outpouring of scholarship since World War II has been remarkable. What have we learned about this medieval institution as a result of so much contemporary scholarly attention? Have we been able to unravel some of the puzzles that legislatures present? Does it matter whether we can do so?

There are over four times as many legislatures in the world today as there were at the end of World War II in 1945, the result of the multiplication of independent national states. This reflects the commitment of nearly every country in the world to having a legislature, if only to perform symbolic functions. Apart from those that serve primarily as instruments for legitimating authoritarian regimes, in three-fifths of the world's democratic political systems, legislatures have broad importance. Two-thirds of democratic legislatures exist in parliamentary systems in which they are usually the only elected institutions of the national government. But as we have seen, this astonishingly broad commitment to legislatures does not mean that they are popular or indeed that they are well understood. Among scholars there has been considerable agreement on how to explain the apparent contradictions that legislatures exhibit. Historians have found explanations in the adaptation of this originally medieval institution to a succession of later social, economic, and political environments. Constitutional lawyers explain the institution in terms of its inherited rules and regulations. Sociologists explain it in terms of the role conceptions of legislators. Political scientists explain it in terms of the strategies and tactics pursued by members to achieve political goals. But scholarly explanations have largely remained the province of the communities that produced them. Worse, the explanations are to some extent isolated from each other by the separation of scholarly disciplines and the separation among scholars of different nations. For journalists, interested observers, and the broader public, the result of all the research that has been done is a large body of new information on legislatures, often lifted out of its theoretical context and therefore subject to lots of different interpretations and purposes. This means that facts are more readily available to support the various criticisms of legislatures that surface frequently everywhere. Scholarship has not produced wider understanding of this institution, in large part because it exists outside the experience of most people. It is not at all like the business, religious, educational, or volunteer organizations relevant to the lives and work of most people.

Findings of Scholarship

To consider whether scholarship has improved public understanding, we can review the principal conclusions produced by recent research in six areas.

The Role of Committees Versus the Role of Parties

The study of committees and party organization within legislatures has provided a set of competing hypotheses about whether legislative committees are instruments of legislative parties or are autonomous centers of the influence of special interests within their fields of jurisdiction. The tentative conclusion of research is that political parties control the committees, both in the U.S. Congress and in the German Bundestag, the two legislatures with the most highly developed committee systems. Parties, when they are cohesive, find that committees are effective instruments enabling them to achieve their policy objectives in separate areas without having to reconcile them on the floor of the chamber. Research on committees has provided an explanation of their early origin in legislatures and their purposes by showing that committees provide a framework for bargaining among members, which imposes discipline on those bargains so that they will stick. Committees also provide specialized information unavailable to the chamber as a whole. Research on committees has revised the conclusion held thirty years ago that parties and committees are alternative ways of organizing legislatures, that when committees are strong, legislative parties tend to be weak, and vice versa. Instead, accumulated evidence demonstrates that parties and committees can act in concert and not in place of each other. Furthermore, formal modeling has offered insights into the sources of committee power in the sequence of the legislative process.

The Influence of Constituencies

Research on the linkages between constituencies and their representatives has shown that constituency influence is strong in the decentralized party systems of the United States and developing countries and much weaker where parties are centralized and there are multimember constituencies. Constituency influence, where it exists, is strongest on those relatively few national issues that attract public attention and on local needs and concerns. The increasing cohesiveness of political parties in the United States has not diminished the influence of constituencies on legislators. That surprising outcome results from a realignment of party majorities in American congressional districts, the consequence of the civil rights movement, which eroded Democratic Party support in the South and Republican support in the Northeast. As a consequence, political regions in the United States have become relatively homogeneous, making it possible to speak of "blue states" and "red states," and within these regions the political composition of constituencies is remarkably one-sided. This specifically American example of the sources of party cohesion has reminded us that the single-member-constituency system for electing legislators does not necessarily create party fractionalization in the legislature. Internal party divisions have existed during some periods of American history, notably during the time of "the textbook Congress," and in some countries in Africa and Latin America, but party cohesion is affected by a variety of influences and not by electoral systems alone.

The Reason for Restrictive Procedures

Formal modeling of the rules that structure decision making has greatly clarified the function of restrictive procedures in legislatures. It has demonstrated both the rationale for the rules and their impact on decisions. It has modeled the legislative process as a strategic game whose rules shape outcomes. It takes account both of legislators' preferences as they seek to achieve their objectives and of the institutional structure of the legislature that constrains their actions. This research provides explanations for how legislatures avoid being overwhelmed by the large number of political issues generated in most societies, how they avoid the chaos that can easily result in endless voting cycles because of the existence of multiple majorities on many issues, and how they achieve agreement on a sequence of decision making. Game theory has revived interest in the structure of the institution, which had been neglected by the micropolitical approach encouraged by the "behavioral persuasion" in political science.

Executive-Legislative Relations

Theories of legislative-executive relations, cabinet stability, and presidential influence in legislatures have been formulated and tested with extensive data. This research has led to conditional conclusions about the circumstances under which cabinets survive or fall and the circumstances that give presidents leverage over legislative decisions. Studies of cabinet durability have compared the influence of formative factors related to the appointment and composition of the cabinet with the impact of unpredictable "external shocks." Research on presidential influence has detailed the effect of electoral factors—presidential "coattails"—on relative executive-legislative influence and has examined the interplay of "veto bargaining." This area of research has provided explanations of the sources and consequences of "divided government" and "legislative gridlock," placing these conditions in the broader perspective of bargaining in the legislative process. It has shown that these conditions are not the distinctive result of the separation of legislative and executive branches in the United States but have their counterpart in the German parliamentary system in the form of conflict between Bundestag and Bundesrat and in the French hybrid system in the form of "cohabitation."

The Paradox of Public Attitudes Toward Legislators and Legislatures

Research on public attitudes toward legislatures has ranged broadly, providing evidence that general economic conditions and specific issues affect public evaluations of the institution across time and nations. Research has explained the reasons for the difference between attitudes toward individual members and toward the collective membership and has distinguished between attitudes toward the legislative process and toward legislative policy outcomes. One plausible generalization derived from a range of studies on public perceptions of the legislature is that legislatures mirror the public's disagreements on issues. Legislatures constantly demonstrate that there is no easily discovered solution to most political issues and that the prospect of consensus on issues is often an illusion. The public therefore projects on the legislature its unwillingness to face dissensus and its despair about finding solutions. None of the more popular institutions of government provide similar mirrors to the reality of political controversy.

The Development of Legislatures

The study of the development of legislatures through time has occupied some historians continuously but has been relatively rare in political science until recently. Political scientists investigating the history of legislatures have formulated theories of "institutionalization," of the influences that set legislatures clearly apart from the rest of the system of government, give their organization a distinctive, complex structure, and shape the careers of their members. Nelson Polsby's 1968 study of the institutionalization of the U.S. House of Representatives became a template for others, and as work has proceeded, measures of institutionalization applicable to other legislatures have been developed.[1] The institutionalization of legislatures is more clearly understood than is the relationship between the development of legislatures and democratization. Interesting work has, however, been done on the development of legislatures in particular settings, making use of the concepts of contingent beginnings and of path dependence in their adaptations over time. The study of the historical evolution of legislatures provides useful clues to resolving some of the puzzles that legislatures exhibit: The history of the institution reveals the contrast between its origins and the result of its successive adaptations.

Research with a historical dimension has produced an ever greater recognition among scholars of legislatures' varying functions in increasingly complicated societies and their performance of these functions. Attracting extraordinary scholarly interest in the last half century are the apparent indispensability of legislatures in political systems, their proliferation worldwide, their accessibility to research, and their centrality in politics. Research in many other areas of political science—voting behavior, cabinet stability, executive authority, bureaucratic autonomy, federalism—often connects to legislatures. But scholarly attention has not solved the most persistent puzzle that legislatures present: how to improve the public's understanding of the institution designed to represent it.

A Case Study of the Problem of Legislature-Public Linkage

An example of congressional deliberation on a salient issue in the United States, the reform of health care, demonstrates how an intrinsically complicated issue can become additionally confounded because the legislative process baffles the public. The issue, which attracted repeated public attention in every decade of the second half of the twentieth century, was on the congressional agenda again in the first decade of the twenty-first century. Public opinion on the need for reform was divided in a complex manner. Age and income, more than partisan preference, influenced both support for and opposition to reform.[2] But congressional leaders had an interest in dividing their members along party lines, even though that division did not accurately mirror public opinion. Members of Congress had an incentive to attribute their opposing views to the views of their constituents, but to some extent this required distortion. Since congressional party leaders were the most prominent protagonists in the controversy, the public suspected that the controversy primarily reflected partisan interests. And since the president made his own proposal late in the legislative process, the final decision could appear to be a referendum on the president rather than the product of a long-standing policy controversy. In these respects, large sectors of the public did not recognize their views in the debate on the issue in Congress, contributing to public cynicism over the way the issue was being discussed there.

The complexity and length of the fourteen-month legislative process that took place in 2009 and 2010 added to public frustration. The health-care reform bills were considered by three committees in the House of Representatives and two in the Senate, exhibiting the puzzling decentralization of congressional organization and the problem of coordination. The assignment to these five committees reflected the strategy of the congressional sponsors of the reform legislation, who hoped to achieve bipartisan support in the Senate Finance Committee and compromise among the divided views of Democratic members in the three House committees. But this legislative strategy was obscure to the wider public. The president and the congressional leaders of the reform effort took the views of major hospital, pharmaceutical, and doctor groups conspicuously into account in order to generate support in the constituencies of recalcitrant members. In public it looked like they were making concessions to special interests.[3] Restrictive procedures were frequently on display in the constraints imposed on debate in the House of Representatives by the Speaker acting with the Rules Committee and in the constant threat of a filibuster to prevent majority decisions in the Senate. The achievement of agreement between House and Senate versions of the final legislation through the use of an unfamiliar "reconciliation procedure" gave the ruling of the Senate parliamentarians unusual prominence and exposed the process to the charge of illegitimate manipulation.[4] In these ways the legislative process in Congress obscured the substance of the controversy over health-care reform by overlaying it with the display of just those legislative processes that puzzle and dismay the general public.

The Problem of Translating Research Findings into Public Understanding

Making the legislative process difficult to understand is the fact that the actions of the individuals who make up the legislature are readily observable and comprehensible, while its organization and procedures are not. Legislative research in the last half century has focused both on the members of the institution, as a result of the "behavioral persuasion" in political science, and on the structure of the institution, as a result of the game-theoretical approach. Putting these two approaches together to understand the institution recalls what Eulau called "the micro-macro dilemma" in political science, which consists of distinguishing between units of observation and units of analysis, as well as the problem of using individual-level observations (say, of members) to measure aggregate properties (say, of legislative processes). This general methodological dilemma has special applicability to the study of the institution of the legislature, since it is so obviously composed of individual members and their constituencies, and yet so obviously has collective properties—rules, structures, developmental history, cultural contexts—that are more than the sum of members or constituencies. The point is that this is not only a methodological dilemma but one that affects public understanding of the institution.

It is much more natural for nonprofessional observers of legislatures to focus on their individual members rather than on their collective properties. Public discussions of legislatures easily devolve into discussions of the strengths and foibles of individual members or debate about their policy positions. To the extent that the public pays attention to the legislative institution as a whole, discussions easily sink into ridicule of the seemingly mysterious procedures that legislatures have developed to enable them to transform the positions of their large memberships into decisions of the whole body. Individual legislators are readily observed and subject to discussion; the collective properties of legislatures, being relatively abstract, are not casually observable.

Does it matter that the public fails to understand the legislature? After all, that failure has not endangered the survival of legislatures. Public frustration with Congress due to its long deliberation over major issues such as health-care reform has not led to a proposal to abolish Congress; nor have there been significant movements to abolish legislatures anywhere else in the world, either where they are relatively new or where they have long histories. But as the case of health-care reform in the United States illustrates, the public's failure to understand legislatures obscures the real political issues that legislatures deal with; frustrated with how legislatures deal with issues, the public becomes distracted from differences of opinion about the issues themselves. The failure to understand the legislative institution invites the conclusion that were it not for the convolutions of the legislative process, big issues could be readily resolved. And while this is nothing new, the extent of demands for solutions to economic and social issues in both the developing and advanced industrialized democracies confronts legislatures with possibly the greatest volume of policy challenges they have ever faced. Unfortunately, the remarkable attention to legislatures by scholars in the last half century has done little to explain the institution outside the academy.

The performance of legislatures' original function, that of linking government to its citizens, results in one of the most consequential differences among political systems—between those that base government on broad consultation and those that rely on coercion. Since legislatures have become ubiquitous, their mere existence does not assure that governments are consultative. Determining how consultative they are, and how they consult, is the task of legislative research. In finding new evidence of what legislatures do, research has reduced the puzzle of how this old institution has been adapted to the needs of modern and modernizing political systems. But the challenge of explaining the legislature to an audience beyond the academic professionals interested in it remains unmet. Doing so requires collaboration between academic scholarship, teacher education, and political journalism. The incentives for that collaboration are unfortunately weak. Its importance is, however, strong, especially in a time of high public expectations of government and low confidence in its performance.

NOTES

Chapter One

1. Inter-Parliamentary Union website: www.ipu.org/parline-e/ParliamentsStructure.asp?REGION=All&LANG=ENG.

2. M. Steven Fish and Matthew Kroenig, *The Handbook of National Legislatures: A Global Survey* (Cambridge: Cambridge University Press, 2009).

3. Samuel P. Huntington, *The Third Wave: Democratization in the Late Twentieth Century* (Norman: University of Oklahoma Press, 1991).

4. Woodrow Wilson, *Congressional Government: A Study in American Politics* (Boston, MA: Houghton Mifflin, 1885).

5. Nelson W. Polsby and Eric Schickler, "Landmarks in the Study of Congress Since 1945," *Annual Review of Political Science* 5 (2002): 333–367.

6. Brian F. Crisp and Felipe Botero, "Multicountry Studies of Latin American Legislatures: A Review Article," *Legislative Studies Quarterly* 29 (2004): 329–356.

7. The History of Parliament website: www.histparl.ac.uk.

8. Helen M. Cam, "The International Commission for the History of Representative and Parliamentary Institutions," *Parliamentary Affairs* 9 (1955): 490–493; John Rogister, "The International Commission for the History of Representative and Parliamentary Institutions: Aims and Achievements over 70 Years," *Parliaments, Estates & Representation* 27 (2007): 1–7. See also www.ichrpi.org.

9. Kommission für Geschichte des Parlamentarismus und der politischen Parteien website: www.kgparl.de/publi-editionen.html.

10. William O. Aydelotte, ed., *The History of Parliamentary Behavior* (Princeton, NJ: Princeton University Press, 1977).

11. Richard F. Fenno Jr., "If, As Ralph Nader Says, Congress Is the 'Broken Branch,' How Come We Love Our Congressmen So Much?" in *Congress in Change: Evolution and Reform*, ed. Norman Ornstein (New York: Praeger, 1975), 286.

12. Antonio Marongiu, *Medieval Parliaments: A Comparative Study* (London: Eyre & Spottiswoode, 1968), parts 1 and 2.

13. Lord Campion, *An Introduction to the Procedure of the House of Commons*, 3rd ed. (London: Macmillan, 1958), ch. 1.

14. Jack P. Greene, *The Quest for Power: The Lower Houses of Assembly in the Southern Royal Colonies, 1689–1776* (Chapel Hill: University of North Carolina Press, 1963); Michael Kammen, *Deputyes and Libertyes: The Origins of Representative Government in Colonial America* (New York: Knopf, 1969).

15. Peverill Squire and Keith E. Hamm, *101 Chambers: Congress, State Legislatures, and the Future of Legislative Studies* (Columbus: Ohio State University Press, 2005), ch. 1; Peverill Squire, "Historical Evolution of Legislatures in the United States," *Annual Review of Political Science* 9 (2006): 19–44; Peverill Squire, "The Evolution of American Colonial Assemblies As Legislative Organizations," *Congress & the Presidency* 32 (2005): 109–131.

16. Walter Bagehot, *The English Constitution* (1867; rpt. Cambridge: Cambridge University Press, 2001).

17. Wilson, *Congressional Government*.

18. James Bryce, *Modern Democracies* (London: Macmillan, 1921).

19. James Bryce, "The Decline of Legislatures," in *Modern Democracies* (London: Macmillan, 1921), 335, 338–339.

20. Moisei Ostrogorski, *Democracy and the Organization of Political Parties* (London: Macmillan Company, 1902).

21. Max Weber, "Politik als Beruf" (1918), in *Gesammelte Politische Schriften*, ed. Johannes Winckelmann, 5th ed. (Tübingen: J. C. B. Mohr, 1988), 505–560; Robert Michels, *Political Parties* (New York: Dover Publications, 1959), part 6.

22. Sir Lewis B. Namier, *The Structure of Politics at the Accession of George III* (London: Macmillan, 1929).

23. Ivor Jennings, *Parliament*, 2nd ed. (Cambridge: Cambridge University Press, 1957), 268.

24. Squire and Hamm, *101 Chambers*, 12–13.

25. James S. Young, *The Washington Community, 1800–1828* (New York: Columbia University Press, 1966).

26. *The Federalist* #10.

27. Thomas Jefferson, *A Manual of Parliamentary Practice, Composed Originally for the United States Senate*, 2nd ed. (Washington, DC: John Milligan and William Cooper, 1812).

28. John Hatsell, *Precedents of Proceedings in the House of Commons, with Observations* (London: L. Hansard & Son, 1818).

29. *Oxford English Dictionary*, 2nd ed. (Oxford: Oxford University Press, 1989).

30. Information that the term *legislature* came into usage in this country so soon after it appeared in Great Britain derives from the research on colonial legislatures carried out by Peverill Squire.

31. Nelson W. Polsby, "Legislatures," in *Handbook of Political Science*, ed. F. I. Greenstein and N. W. Polsby, vol. 5 (Reading, MA: Addison-Wesley, 1975), 277–278.

32. Winston Churchill, 393 H. C. Deb. 5th ser., col. 404 (October 28): 1.

Chapter Two

1. Antonio Marongiu, *Medieval Parliaments: A Comparative Study* (London: Eyre & Spottiswoode, 1968), 56.

2. Hanna Pitkin, *The Concept of Representation* (Berkeley, CA: University of California Press), 8–9.

3. Ernest Barker, "Burke and His Bristol Constituency, 1774–1780," in *Essays on Government*, 2nd. ed. (Oxford: Clarendon Press, 1951), 154–204.

4. Werner Patzelt, "Recruitment and Retention in Western European Parliaments," in *Legislatures: Comparative Perspectives on Representative Assemblies*, ed. Gerhard Loewenberg, Peverill Squire, and D. Roderick Kiewiet (Ann Arbor: University Michigan Press, 2002), 80–118; Heinrich Best and Maurizio Cotta, eds., *Parliamentary Representatives in Europe, 1848–2000: Legislative Recruitment and Careers in Eleven European Countries* (Oxford: Oxford University Press, 2000); Heinrich Best and Maurizio Cotta, eds., *Democratic Representation in Europe: Diversity, Change and Convergence* (Oxford: Oxford University Press, 2007).

5. Norman J. Ornstein, Thomas E. Mann, and Michael J. Malbin, eds., *Vital Statistics on Congress 2008* (Washington, DC: Brookings Institution Press, 2008), 35–40.

6. Rob Salmond, "Proportional Representation and Female Parliamentarians: Examining Over-Time Change," *Legislative Studies Quarterly* 31 (2006): 175–204.

7. Ornstein, Mann, and Malbin, *Vital Statistics*, 45.

8. The Inter-Parliamentary Union maintains a running total of women in parliaments; see www.ipu.org/wmn-e/classif.htm.

9. David T. Canon, *Race, Redistricting, and Representation: The Unintended Consequences of Black Majority Districts* (Chicago: University of Chicago Press, 1999), 1–3.

10. Canon, *Race*, 143–200.

11. John C. Wahlke, "Policy Determinants and Legislative Decisions," in *The Politics of Representation: Continuities in Theory and Research*, ed. Heinz Eulau and John C. Wahlke (Beverly Hills, CA: Sage, 1978), 156.

12. Michael L. Mezey, *Representative Democracy: Legislators and Their Constituents* (Lanham, MD: Rowman & Littlefield, 2008), 39.

13. Pitkin, *The Concept of Representation*, 221, 227, 209, respectively.

14. Andrew Rehfeld, "Representation Rethought: On Trustees, Delegates, and Gyroscopes in the Study of Political Representation and Democracy," *American Political Science Review* 103 (May 2009): 221.

15. John C. Wahlke, Heinz Eulau, William Buchanan, and Leroy C. Ferguson, *The Legislative System: Explorations in Legislative Behavior* (New York: John Wiley, 1962), 12.

16. Heinz Eulau, John C. Wahlke, William Buchanan, and Leroy C. Ferguson, "The Role of the Representative: Some Empirical Observations on the Theory of Edmund Burke," *The American Political Science Review* 53 (September 1959): 742–756.

17. Warren E. Miller and Donald E. Stokes, "Constituency Influence in Congress," *The American Political Science Review* 57 (1963): 45–56.

18. Miller and Stokes, "Constituency Influence in Congress," 51–53.

19. Malcolm E. Jewell and Gerhard Loewenberg, "Editors' Introduction: Toward a New Model of Legislative Representation," *Legislative Studies Quarterly* 4 (1979): 485–499.

20. Paul D. Karps and Heinz Eulau, "Policy Representation As an Emergent: Toward a Situational Analysis," in *The Politics of Representation: Continuities in Theory and Research*, ed. Heinz Eulau and John C. Wahlke (Beverly Hills, CA: Sage, 1978), 207–231.

21. Robert L. Hall, *Participation in Congress* (New Haven, CT: Yale University Press, 1996), 239–240.

22. Heinz Eulau and Kenneth Prewitt, *Labyrinths of Democracy: Adaptations, Linkages, Representation and Policies in Urban Politics* (Indianapolis: Bobbs-Merrill, 1973).

23. Eulau and Prewitt, *Labyrinths of Democracy*, 424.

24. David R. Mayhew, *Congress: The Electoral Connection* (New Haven, CT: Yale University Press, 1974).

25. Richard F. Fenno Jr., *Home Style: House Members in Their Districts* (Boston, MA: Little, Brown, 1978).

26. Gary C. Jacobsen, "The Persistence of Democratic House Majorities," in *The Electoral Origins of Divided Government: Competition in U.S. House Elections, 1946–1988*, ed. Gary W. Cox and Samuel Kernell (Boulder, CO: Westview Press, 1990), 59–84; Gary C. Jacobsen, *The Politics of Congressional Elections* (New York: Pearson/Longman, 2009).

27. William Robert Clark, Matt Golder, and Sona Nadenichek Golder, *Principles of Comparative Politics* (Washington, DC: CQ Press, 2009), 517–522.

28. Clark, Golder, and Golder, *Principles*, 713.

29. Warren E. Miller, *Policy Representation in Western Democracies* (New York: Oxford University Press, 1999).

30. Bernhard Wessels, "System Characteristics Matter: Empirical Evidence from Ten Representation Studies," in *Policy Representation in Western Democracies*, ed. Warren E. Miller, Roy Pierce, Jacques Thomassen, and Richard Herrera (New York: Oxford University Press, 1999), 137–161.

31. G. Bingham Powell Jr., "Political Representation in Comparative Politics," *Annual Review of Political Science* 7 (2004): 273–296.

32. Anthony Downs, *An Economic Theory of Democracy* (New York: Harper & Row, 1957).

33. Keith Poole and Howard Rosenthal, *Congress: A Political-Economic History of Roll Call Voting* (New York: Oxford University Press, 1997).

34. Christopher J. Kam, *Party Discipline and Parliamentary Politics* (Cambridge: Cambridge University Press, 2009).

35. Gerhard Loewenberg, "The Contribution of Comparative Research to Measuring the Policy Preferences of Legislators," *Legislative Studies Quarterly* 33 (2008): 499–510.

Chapter Three

1. J. E. Neale, *The Elizabethan House of Commons* (Hammondsworth, UK: Penguin, 1963), 133.

2. Peverill Squire, "Historical Evolution of Legislatures in the United States," *Annual Review of Political Science* 9 (2006): 24–25.

3. Peverill Squire and Keith E. Hamm, *101 Chambers: Congress, State Legislatures, and the Future of Legislative Studies* (Columbus: Ohio State University Press, 2005), 13.

4. Quoted in Rick K. Wilson, "Transitional Governance in the United States: Lessons from the First Continental Congress," in *Legislatures: Comparative Perspectives on Representative Assemblies*, ed. Gerhard Loewenberg, Peverill Squire, and D. Roderick Kiewiet (Ann Arbor: University of Michigan Press), 299–300.

5. Wilson, "Transitional Governance," 297.

6. Squire and Hamm, *101 Chambers*, 6.

7. Calvin Jillson and Rick K. Wilson, *Congressional Dynamics: Structure, Coordination, and Choice in the First American Congress, 1774–1789* (Stanford, CA: Stanford University Press, 1994).

8. John Hatsell, *Precedents of Proceedings in the House of Commons, with Observations* (London: L. Hansard & Son, 1818).

9. Thomas Erskine May, *A Treatise on the Law, Privileges, Proceedings and Usage of Parliament* (London: W. Clowes and Sons, 1906).

10. Until 1967 the only German compilation of parliamentary procedure was one volume of a projected two-volume work by Julius Hatschek, *Das Parlamentsrecht des Deutschen Reiches* (Berlin and Leipzig: G. J. Goschen'sche Verlagshandlung, 1915). Since then there is Hans Trossman, *Parlamentsrecht und Praxis des deutschen Bundestages* (Bonn: Stollfuss-Verlag, 1966), and Hans-Peter Schneider und Wolfgang Zeh, eds., *Parlamentsrecht und Parlamentspraxis* (Berlin: Walter deGruyter, 1989).

11. John Bowring, ed., *The Works of Jeremy Bentham* (Edinburgh: Tait, 1848), 2: 299–373.

12. Wolfgang Zeh, "Parlamentarische Strukturen als Exportartikel: Ein Essay Über Chancen und Grenzen der Beratung in Demokratisierungsprozessen," in *Parlamentarismusforschung in Deutschland*, ed. Helmar Schöne and Julia von Blumenthal (Baden-Baden: Nomos, 2009), 80–81.

13. Gerhard Loewenberg, *Parliament in the German Political System* (Ithaca, NY: Cornell University Press, 1967), 8–9; Gerhard Loewenberg and Samuel C. Patterson, *Comparing Legislatures* (Boston: Little, Brown, 1979), 13–19.

14. Zeh, "Parlamentarische Strukturen als Exportartikel," 77–92.

15. Gerhard Loewenberg, "The Influence of Congressional Hearings on Committee Procedure in the German Bundestag," in *Exporting Congress? The Influence of the U.S. Congress on World Legislatures*, ed. Timothy J. Power and Nicol C. Rae (Pittsburgh, PA: University of Pittsburgh Press, 2006), 102–118; cf. Michael F. Feldkamp, "Karl Mom-

mer und die Anfänge des deutschen Bundestages," in Schöne and von Blumenthal, *Parlamentarismusforschung in Deutschland*, 231–256.

16. John D. Huber, *Rationalizing Parliament: Legislative Institutions and Party Politics in France* (Cambridge: Cambridge University Press, 1996), 2–7.

17. Adolf Kimmel, "Stärkung der 'Hyperpräsidentschaft' oder Emanzipation des Parlaments? Die französische Verfassungsänderung vom 23. Juli 2008," *Zeitschrift für Parlamentsfragen* 39 (2008): 849–866.

18. U.S. Constitution, art. 1, sec. 5, para. 2.

19. Peverill Squire, "Territorial Legislatures As the Missing Link," unpublished manuscript, 2010, citing Howard Roberts Lamar, *Dakota Territory, 1861–1889: A Study of Frontier Politics* (New Haven, CT: Yale University Press, 1956), 85–86, and Bartlett Tripp and John Henry Worst, "Territory of Dakota," in *The Province and the States*, ed. Weston Arthur Goodspeed, vol. 6 (Madison, WI: Western Historical Society, 1904), 228–229.

20. Kenneth A. Shepsle and Barry R. Weingast, eds., "Positive Theories of Congressional Institutions," in *Positive Theories of Congressional Institutions* (Ann Arbor: University of Michigan Press, 1995), 5–35.

21. Helmar Schöne, *Alltag im Parlament: Parlamentskultur in Theorie und Empirie* (Baden-Baden: Nomos, 2010), 231–245.

22. William H. Riker, *Agenda Formation* (Ann Arbor: University of Michigan Press, 1993), 2.

23. Gary W. Cox and Mathew D. McCubbins, *Setting the Agenda: Responsible Party Government in the U.S. House of Representatives* (Cambridge: Cambridge University Press, 2005).

24. Tracy H. Slagter and Gerhard Loewenberg, "Path Dependence As an Explanation of the Institutional Stability of the German Parliament," *German Politics* 18 (2009): 473–474, 477–478.

25. Huber, *Rationalizing Parliament*, 33, 89–92.

26. Gary Cox, William B. Heller, and Mathew McCubbins, "Agenda Power in the Italian Chamber of Deputies, 1988–2000," *Legislative Studies Quarterly* 33 (2008): 171–198.

27. Scott Morgenstern, "Explaining Legislative Politics in Latin America," in *Legislative Politics in Latin America*, ed. Scott Morgenstern and Benito Nacif (Cambridge: Cambridge University Press, 2002), 414.

28. Gary W. Cox and Scott Morgenstern, "Epilogue: Latin America's Reactive Assemblies and Proactive Presidents," in Morgenstern and Nacif, *Legislative Politics in Latin America*, 459, 465.

29. *The Federalist* #10.

30. Heinrich Best, "'Disorder Yields to Order Fair the Place': The Emergence of Political Parties in Western and Central Europe," *Parliaments, Estates & Representation* 15 (1995): 133–145.

31. Kaare Strom, Wolfgang C. Mueller, and Daniel Markham Smith, "Parliamentary Control of Coalition Governments," *Annual Review of Political Science* 13 (May 2010): 517–535.

32. David Williams, *Condorcet and Modernity* (Cambridge: Cambridge University Press, 2004), 206–212.

33. Kenneth J. Arrow, *Social Choice and Individual Values* (New York: Wiley, 1951).

34. Bjørn Erik Rasch, "Parliamentary Floor Voting Procedures and Agenda Setting in Europe" in Loewenberg, Squire, and Kiewiet, *Legislatures*, 270–276.

35. George Tsbelis and Jeannette Money, *Bicameralism* (Cambridge: Cambridge University Press, 1997), ch. 4.

36. Kenneth Shepsle and Barry R. Weingast, "The Institutional Foundations of Committee Power," *The American Political Science Review* 81 (March 1987): 85–104.

37. Matthias Lehnert, "Der Einfluss der Parteipolitik auf das Vermittlungsverfahren: Eine Analyse der Einigungsvorschläge (1949–2005)," in Schöne and von Blumenthal, *Parlamentarismusforschung in Deutschland*, 279–299.

38. U.S. Constitution, art. 5.

39. George Tsebelis, *Veto Players: How Political Institutions Work* (Princeton, NJ: Princeton University Press, 2002), ch. 7.

Chapter Four

1. Philip E. Converse and Roy Pierce, *Political Representation in France* (Cambridge, MA: Harvard University Press, 1986), ch. 8.

2. John W. Kingdon, "Politicians' Beliefs About Voters," *The American Political Science Review* 61 (March 1967): 137–145.

3. Joel D. Barkan, ed., *Legislative Power in Emerging African Democracies* (Boulder, CO: Lynne Rienner, 2009), 12–15.

4. Diana Mutz and Gregory N. Flemming, "How Good People Make Bad Collectives: A Social-Psychological Perspective on Public Attitudes Toward Congress," in *Congress and the Decline of Public Trust*, ed. Joseph Cooper (Boulder, CO: Westview Press, 1999), 79–99.

5. John D. Huber and Charles R. Shipan, *Deliberate Discretion? The Institutional Foundations of Bureaucratic Autonomy* (Cambridge: Cambridge University Press, 2002), chs. 6–8.

6. Ulrich Sieberer, "Können ja—Wollen nein? Die Anreize ausserparlamentarischer Amtsträger zur Beschränkung der Regierung," in *Parlamentarismusforschung in Deutschland,* ed. Helmar Schöne and Julia von Blumenthal (Baden-Baden: Nomos, 2009), 301–320.

7. Michael Laver and Kenneth Shepsle, *Making and Breaking Governments: Cabinets and Legislatures in Parliamentary Democracies* (Cambridge: Cambridge University Press, 1996), 58.

8. Laver and Shepsle, *Making and Breaking Governments,* 66.

9. Christopher J. Kam, *Party Discipline and Parliamentary Politics* (Cambridge: Cambridge University Press, 2009).

10. Michael Laver, "Government Termination," *Annual Review of Political Science* 6 (2002): 23–40.

11. Carol Mershon, *The Costs of Coalition* (Stanford, CA: Stanford University Press, 2002).

12. For a good overview, see Matthew Soberg Shugart and John M. Carey, *Presidents and Assemblies: Constitutional Design and Electoral Dynamics* (Cambridge: Cambridge University Press, 1992).

13. Cindy Skach, *Borrowing Constitutional Designs: Constitutional Law in Weimar Germany and the Fifth French Republic* (Princeton, NJ: Princeton University Press, 2005).

14. Gary W. Cox and Scott Morgenstern, "Epilogue: Latin America's Reactive Assemblies and Proactive Presidents," in *Legislative Politics in Latin America,* ed. Scott Morgenstern and Benito Nacif (Cambridge: Cambridge University Press, 2002), 446–468.

15. William Roberts Clark, Matt Golder, and Sona Nadenichek, *Principles of Comparative Politics* (Washington, DC: CQ Press, 2009), 400–402.

16. John R. Hibbing and Elizabeth Theiss-Morse, *Congress As Public Enemy: Public Attitudes Toward American Political Institutions* (Cambridge: Cambridge University Press, 1995), 37.

17. See the Gallup website: www.gallup.com/poll/127343/Congress-Job-Approval-Rating-Improves-Low.aspx.

18. Sarah H. Binder, *Stalemate: Causes and Consequences of Legislative Gridlock* (Washington, DC: Brookings, 2003), 118.

19. Susan Hattis Roelof, "Public Trust in Parliament—A Comparative Study," Knesset Information Division, May 9, 2006, www.knesset.gov.il/mmm/eng/doc_eng.asp?doc=me01417&type=pdf. See especially pp. 7–15.

20. CESifo DICE Report 2/2007, 71 (available at www.cesifo group.de/portal/page/portal/ifoHome/b-publ/b2journal/40pub ldice/_publdice?item_link=dicereportindex207.htm).

21. Werner J. Patzelt, "Warum verachten die Deutschen ihr Parlament und lieben ihr Verfassungsgericht? Ergebnisse einer vergleichenden demoskopischen Studie," *Zeitschrift für Parlamentsfragen* 36 (2005): 517–538.

22. Gerhard Loewenberg, William Mishler, and Howard Sanborn, "Developing Attachments to New Political Institutions: A Multi-Level Model of Attitude Formation in Post-Communist Europe," *European Political Science Review* 3 (2011): in press.

23. "Ineffectual, Unloved, Exhausted," *The Economist*, March 2, 1985, 40.

24. John Miller, "The Representatives and the Represented in England, 1660–1689," *Parliaments, Estates & Representation* 15 (1995): 125–132.

25. Hibbing and Theiss-Morse, *Congress As Public Enemy*, 61.

26. John R. Hibbing and Elizabeth Theiss-Morse, *Stealth Democracy: Americans' Beliefs About How Government Should Work* (Cambridge: Cambridge University Press, 2002).

27. Helmar Schöne, "Politische Institutionen im Urteil von Lehramtsstudierenden und Lehramtsanwärtern," *Gesellschaft-Wirtschaft-Politik* 1 (2010): 100.

28. Jean-Jacques Rousseau, *On the Social Contract*, bk. 3, ch. 15 (1762), available in Susan Dunn, ed., *The Social Contract and The First and Second Discourses* (New Haven, CT: Yale University Press, 2002), 221.

29. Michael Gallagher and Pier Vincenzo Uleri, eds., *The Referendum Experience in Europe* (London: Macmillan, 1996).

30. Elizabeth R. Gerber, *The Populist Paradox: Interest Group Influence and the Promise of Direct Legislation* (Princeton, NJ: Princeton University Press, 1999), ch. 8 and appendix 1.

31. Mark Baldassare, Dean Bonner, Jennifer Paluch, and Sonja Petek, "Californians and Their Government," Public Policy Institute of California Statewide Survey, September 2009, http://www.ppic.org/content/pubs/survey/S_909MBS.pdf. See especially p. 17.

32. Loewenberg, Mishler, and Sanborn, "Developing Attachments."

33. Barkan, *Legislative Power*, 247–248.

34. Hibbing and Theiss-Morse, *Stealth Democracy*, 162.

35. Robert D. Putnam, *Bowling Alone: The Collapse and Revival of American Community* (New York: Simon & Schuster, 2000), ch. 1.

Chapter Five

1. Allan Kornberg and Lloyd D. Musolf, eds., *Legislatures in Developmental Perspective* (Durham, NC: Duke University Press, 1970); Chong Lim Kim, Joel D. Barkan, Ilter Turan, and Malcolm E. Jewell, *The Legislative Connection: The Politics of Representation in Kenya, Korea, and Turkey* (Durham, NC: Duke University Press, 1984).

2. For one example, see Gerhard Loewenberg, "Editor's Introduction: The Role of Legislatures in Managing Social Conflict," *Legislative Studies Quarterly* 3, no. 1 (February 1978): 1–9.

3. Stuart A. Rice, "Some Applications of Statistical Method to Political Research," *The American Political Science Review* 20 (May 1926): 313–329; Stuart A. Rice, "The Behavior of Legislative Groups: A Method of Measurement," *Political Science Quarterly* 40 (March 1925): 60–72.

4. Nelson Polsby and Eric Schickler, "Landmarks in the Study of Congress Since 1945," *Annual Review of Political Science* 5 (2002): 334.

5. The list of past holders of the Congressional Fellowship is available at https://www.apsanet.org/imgtest/CongressionalFellowsRoll Call.pdf.

6. Ralph K. Huitt and Robert L. Peabody, foreword to *Congressmen in Committees*, by Richard F. Fenno Jr. (Boston: Little, Brown, 1973), vi. A similar foreword by these organizers of the Study of Congress series appeared in each volume.

7. The Study of Congress series was published by Little, Brown and consisted of the following volumes: Lewis A. Froman Jr., *The Congressional Process: Strategies, Rules and Procedures*; Randall B. Ripley, *Majority Party Leadership in Congress*; John S. Saloma III, *Congress and the New Politics*; Charles O. Jones, *The Minority Party in Congress*; John F. Manley, *The Politics of Finance: The House Committee on Ways and Means*; Richard F. Fenno Jr., *Congressmen in Committees*.

8. Heinz Eulau, *The Behavioral Persuasion in Politics* (New York: Random House, 1963), 14.

9. Angus Campbell, Philip E. Converse, Warren E. Miller, and Donald E. Stokes, *The American Voter* (New York: Wiley, 1960).

10. John C. Wahlke, Heinz Eulau, William Buchanan, and Leroy C. Ferguson, *The Legislative System: Explorations in Legislative Behavior* (New York: John Wiley, 1962), 8, 10.

11. Wahlke et al., *The Legislative System*, 17–21.

12. Wahlke et al., *The Legislative System*, 465–504.

13. Wahlke et al., *The Legislative System*, 455–463.

14. Malcolm E. Jewell, "Attitudinal Determinants of Legislative Behavior: The Utility of Role Analysis," in *Legislatures in Developmental*

Perspective, ed. Allan Kornberg and Lloyd D. Musolf (Durham, NC: Duke University Press, 1970), 483–484.

15. Jewell, "Attitudinal Determinants," 494–500.

16. For a summary of role-theoretical research, see Donald Searing, *Westminster's World: Understanding Political Roles* (Cambridge, MA: Harvard University Press, 1994), 8.

17. Jürgen von Oertzen, "Rollentheorie als Werkzeug der Parlamentarismusforschung," in *Parlamentarismusforschung in Deutschland: Ergebnisse und Perspektiven 40 Jahre nach Erscheinen von Gerhard Loewenbergs Standardwerk zum Deutschen Bundestag*, ed. Helmar Schöne and Julia von Blumenthal (Baden-Baden: Nomos, 2009), 228.

18. See, as examples of work on legislatures in other countries, Chan Heng Chee, "The Role of Parliamentary Politicians in Singapore," *Legislative Studies Quarterly* 1 (1976): 423–441; Harold D. Clarke and Richard G. Price, "Parliamentary Experience and Representational Role Orientations in Canada," *Legislative Studies Quarterly* 6 (1981): 373–390; Philip E. Converse and Roy Pierce, "Representative Roles and Legislative Behavior in France," *Legislative Studies Quarterly* 4 (1979): 525–562; Mark Hagger and Martin Wing, "Legislative Roles and Clientele Orientations in the European Parliament," *Legislative Studies Quarterly* 4 (1979): 165–196; David Judge and Gabriella Ilonszki, "Member-Constituency Linkages in the Hungarian Parliament," *Legislative Studies Quarterly* 20 (1995): 161–176; Iqbal Narain and Shashi Lata Puri, "Legislators in an Indian State: A Study of Role Images and the Pattern of Constituency Linkages," *Legislative Studies Quarterly* 1 (1976): 315–330.

19. Searing, *Westminster's World*.

20. Searing, *Westminster's World*, 6–7.

21. Richard F. Fenno Jr., *Home Style: House Members in Their Districts* (Boston, MA: Little, Brown, 1978).

22. Helmar Schöne, "Die teilnehmende Beobachtung als Datenerhebungsmethode in der Politikwissenschaft. Methodolgische Reflexion und Werkstattbericht," *Forum: Qualitative Socialforschung* 4, no. 2 (May 2003): 25.

23. Heinz Eulau, *Micro-Macro Dilemmas in Political Science: Personal Pathways Through Complexity* (Norman: University of Oklahoma Press, 1996).

24. Eulau, *Micro-Macro Dilemmas*, 156, 235.

25. Eulau, *Micro-Macro Dilemmas*, 238.

26. See especially the work of Steven S. Smith and his students, and Stanley Bach of the Congressional Research Service, beginning with Steven S. Smith and Stanley Bach, *Managing Uncertainty in the House of Representatives* (Washington, DC: Brookings Institution, 1988).

See also the work of Larry C. Dodd, who served as a congressional fellow in 1974 and 1975 at the time of the major reform of Congress and found that existing research approaches could not explain the changes he observed firsthand. The evolution of congressional scholarship can be traced through the nine editions of *Congress Reconsidered*, which Dodd coedited with Bruce I. Oppenheimer (Washington, DC: CQ Press, 2008).

27. James G. March and Johan P. Olsen, "The New Institutionalism: Organizational Factors in Political Life," *The American Political Science Review* 78 (September 1984): 734–749.

28. Kenneth A. Shepsle, "Assessing Comparative Legislative Research," in *Legislatures: Comparative Perspectives on Representative Assemblies*, ed. Gerhard Loewenberg, Peverill Squire, and D. Roderick Kiewiet (Ann Arbor: University of Michigan Press, 2002), 390.

29. S. M. Amadae and Bruce Bueno de Mesquita, "The Rochester School: The Origins of Positive Political Theory," *Annual Review of Political Science* 2 (1999): 270.

30. Kenneth A. Shepsle and Barry R. Weingast, eds., *Positive Theories of Congressional Institutions* (Ann Arbor: University of Michigan Press, 1995).

31. Gerald Gamm and John Huber, "Legislatures As Political Institutions: Beyond the Contemporary Congress," in *Political Science: State of the Discipline*, ed. Ira Katznelson and Helen V. Milner (New York: W. W. Norton, 2002), 327.

32. Gary W. Cox, "On the Effects of Legislative Rules," in *Legislatures: Comparative Perspectives on Representative Assemblies*, ed. Gerhard Loewenberg, Peverill Squire, and D. Roderick Kiewiet (Ann Arbor: University of Michigan Press, 2002), 247–268.

33. John D. Huber, "Restrictive Legislative Procedures in France and the United States," *The American Political Science Review* 86 (September 1992): 675–687.

34. Bjørn Erik Rasch, "Floor Voting Procedures and Agenda Setting in Europe," in Loewenberg, Squire, and Kiewiet, *Legislatures*, 269–287.

35. Keith Krehbiel, *Pivotal Politics: A Theory of U.S. Lawmaking* (Chicago: University of Chicago Press, 1998).

36. Brian F. Crisp and Felipe Botero, "Multicountry Studies of Latin American Legislatures: A Review Article," *Legislative Studies Quarterly* 29 (2004): 349–353.

37. Keith Krehbiel, *Information and Legislative Organization* (Ann Arbor: University of Michigan Press, 1992); D. Roderick Kiewiet and Mathew D. McCubbins, *The Logic of Delegation: Congressional Parties and*

the Appropriations Process (Chicago: University of Chicago Press, 1991); Charles M. Cameron, *Veto Bargaining: Presidents and the Politics of Negative Power* (Cambridge: Cambridge University Press, 2000); Gary W. Cox and Mathew D. McCubbins, *Setting the Agenda: Responsible Party Government in the U.S. House of Representatives* (Cambridge: Cambridge University Press, 2005).

38. John D. Huber, *Rationalizing Parliament: Legislative Institutions and Party Politics in France* (Cambridge: Cambridge University Press, 1996); Michael Laver and Kenneth Shepsle, *Making and Breaking Governments: Cabinets and Legislatures in Parliamentary Democracies* (Cambridge: Cambridge University Press, 1996).

39. Carol Mershon, *The Costs of Coalition* (Stanford, CA: Stanford University Press, 2002); Douglas Dion, *Turning the Legislative Thumbscrew: Minority Rights and Procedural Change in Legislative Politics* (Ann Arbor: University of Michigan Press, 1997).

40. Gamm and Huber, "Legislatures As Political Institutions," 327.

41. Barry R. Weingast, "Rational Choice Institutionalism," in *Political Science: The State of the Discipline*, ed. Ira Katznelson and Helen V. Milner (New York: W. W. Norton, 2002), 691.

42. Douglass C. North and Barry R. Weingast, "Constitutions and Commitment: The Evolution of Institutional Governing Public Choice in Seventeenth-Century England," *The Journal of Economic History* 49, no. 4 (December 1989): 803–832; Gary W. Cox, *The Efficient Secret: The Cabinet and the Development of Political Parties in Victorian England* (Cambridge: Cambridge University Press, 1987).

43. Shepsle, "Assessing Comparative Legislative Research," 388.

Chapter Six

1. Nelson Polsby, "The Institutionalization of the U.S. House of Representatives," *The American Political Science Review* 62 (1968): 144–168.

2. David W. Brady and Daniel P. Kessler, "Who Supports Health Reform?" *PS* (January 2010): 1–6.

3. Amy Melissa McKay and Jennifer Hays Clark, "The Politics of Health Reform: How Political Interests and Preferences Shape Political Strategy," *PS* (October 2009): 808–811.

4. "From Under the Radar to Under a Microscope: Senate Rules Expert Becomes Referee of Health Overhaul," *New York Times,* March 14, 2010.

INDEX

About the Author

Gerhard Loewenberg is the University of Iowa Foundation Distinguished Professor of Political Science, emeritus, and director of its Comparative Legislative Research Center. He is the author of *Parliament in the German Political System,* coauthor of *Comparing Legislatures,* coeditor of the *Handbook of Legislative Research,* and author of numerous articles in professional journals. He earned his PhD from Cornell University. Loewenberg is a recipient of the Frank J. Goodnow Award for Distinguished Service from the American Political Science Association and is a fellow of the American Academy of Arts and Sciences. He served as dean of the College of Liberal Arts and Sciences of the University of Iowa and was cochair of the East-West Parliamentary Practice Project, which conducted seminars and workshops for members of the newly democratic parliaments of Central Europe after the collapse of their Communist regimes.